Just O N E Click

Christians, Porn, and the Lure of Cybersex

Robert J. Baird
Ronald L. Vanderbeck

HOPE & HEALING
INSTITUTE

Grand Rapids, Michigan

FAITH
ALIVE®
Christian Resources

Grand Rapids, Michigan

Just One Click: Christians, Porn, and the Lure of Cybersex. Originally published as *Behind Closed Doors: Christians, Pornography, and the Temptations of Cyberspace*. This revised edition is copublished by the Hope and Healing Institute and Faith Alive Christian Resources.

We welcome your comments. Call us at 1-800-333-8300 or e-mail us at editors@faithaliveresources.org.

Note: This book is intended for general information only and is not intended to supplant advice, diagnosis, treatment, or therapy by a personal physician or professional counselor.

Library of Congress Cataloging-in-Publication Data
Baird, Robert J.
    Just one click : Christians, porn, and the lure of cybersex / Robert J. Baird, Ronald L. Vanderbeck. — [Rev. ed.].
        p. cm.
    Rev. ed. of: Behind closed doors.
    Includes bibliographical references (p.   ).
    ISBN 978-1-59255-514-7
    1. Internet pornography—Religious aspects—Christianity. 2. Computer sex—Religious aspects—Christianity. I. Vanderbeck, Ronald L. II. Baird, Robert J. Behind closed doors. III. Title.
    BV4597.6.B35 2010
    241'.66702854678—dc22

                                                    2010005020

10 9 8 7 6 5 4 3 2 1

FSC
Mixed Sources
Product group from well-managed forests, controlled sources and recycled wood or fiber

Cert no. SCS-COC-002464
www.fsc.org
©1996 Forest Stewardship Council

Contents

"Here I am! I stand at the door and knock."   —Revelation 3:20

Preface

I n an age when children and families are at risk of being affected by destructive forms of sexuality and the distortions of pornography, the Hope and Healing Institute is a nondenominational ministry committed to protection, healing, and renewal. The Institute provides an extensive range of services including crisis intervention, clinical counseling, psychological assessment, and forensic consultation. It is dedicated to bringing hope and healing to those who struggle with problems associated with pornography, cybersex, sexual abuse, incest, infidelity, or sexual addiction. The Institute is a sanctuary of solace and healing for those who have been victimized and a place where strugglers experience the redemptive grace of Jesus Christ.

The Institute has one fundamental goal: to unite the worldwide faith community to be more proactive in combating the proliferation of pornography and the exploitation of children, adolescents, and adults

Please visit www.hopeandhealinginstitute.com for more information.

Chapter 1

An Invitation to Renewal and Restoration

Tim's wife had only been gone for a minute or so. As usual he had given her a peck on the cheek, wished her a good day, and waved goodbye. He waited to boot up his computer until she had pulled out of the driveway. Ever since he'd gotten his new computer he looked forward to her leaving for work. It's not that he didn't love her; he truly did. But this was time for him to do something he wouldn't conceive of doing when she was at home. He closed the door to the den and removed last night's Bible study notes from his chair. It didn't take him long to get comfortable and find his favorite sites. He was so immersed in what he was doing that he never heard the door open. His heartbroken wife stood speechless.

John graduated toward the top of his class in law school and was quickly recruited by a prestigious firm. With a private office, a personal secretary, and law clerks to assist him, he had all the resources to be a successful attorney. He always arrived early and was one of the last to leave. So the senior partners could not understand why his billings were so low.

But John wasn't working on briefs when he was behind the closed doors of his office.

Kate considered herself a typical soccer mom. Her husband had a good paying job so she didn't have to work. She carted her three kids around to school and sporting events. By all appearances she seemed to have the perfect life. Nice husband. Great kids. Big house. But Kate was bored. Her husband spent so many hours at work that she didn't feel her needs were being met. So Kate turned to Internet chatrooms. She wasn't looking primarily for sex. What she craved was affirmation and affection. There she found the attention she sought.

Stephen was a sophomore in high school. His parents took him to see a psychologist who specializes in adolescent depression. Stephen had all the telltale signs of depression: he was sleeping through all of his classes at school; he was no longer hanging out with his friends; he used to be an avid soccer player, but not any more. Clinically speaking, he was depressed. But what his parents didn't know was that after they went to bed at night, Stephen would quietly boot up his computer and surf through porn sites till the wee hours of the morning.

Jill was in middle school—eighth grade, to be exact. When her parents came to the offices of The Hope and Healing Institute, both of their faces were ashen. Her father's hands trembled as he described the pictures they'd found on their daughter's digital camera—pictures of Jill and her boyfriend. They had met in their church's youth group. What should have been a story of puppy love instead escalated into a story of coercion. The boyfriend had introduced Jill to the world of "virtual" reality, where reality quickly becomes distorted. Jill truly believed that what she encountered there represented normal relationships. She had nothing to base her conclusion on, since sex was never openly discussed in her home.

I f any of these stories sounds familiar to you, it's not surprising. Statistics show that one in five Americans uses the Internet to look for pornography or engage in cybersexual "chat." In fact, sex is the most frequently searched topic on the Internet—more than games, music, travel, jokes, cars, jobs, weather, and health material combined.[1] In a recent survey, one in ten people reported believing he or she was addicted to sex via the Internet. Moreover, one in four disclosed feeling that on at least one occasion his or her online sexual behavior was out of control.[2]

A survey conducted by Focus on the Family with Zogby International indicates that one out of five American adults may have looked for sex on the Internet. Twenty percent of the respondents admitted to having visited a sexually oriented website (representing approximately 40 million adults). Nearly 26 percent of men and 17 percent of women indicated that it was either somewhat or very likely that the Internet is capable of providing sexual fulfillment. Not sexual stimulation; sexual fulfillment.[3]

Rabbit Hunting and the Proliferation of Porn

In 1953 an event took place that would forever change the moral complexion of American society: the publication of *Playboy* magazine. With his bunny insignia and Playboy Play-mates, Hugh Hefner introduced pornography into mainstream American culture. What had earlier been shunned or ridiculed was soon to become not only tolerated but also celebrated. Prior to *Playboy*, the public perception was that users of porn were perverted or twisted. Hefner, however, marketed his material in such a way that his readers could consider themselves sophisticated, intelligent, and debonair. In a very real way, pornography became fashionable. No longer hidden in back alleys, pornography was readily available at newsstands and delivered by the United States Postal Service.

9

The popularity of Hefner's product was enormous, and for nearly fifteen years Playboy Enterprises monopolized the market. Then, in 1969, an advertisement appeared in the *New York Times*. It featured the *Playboy* bunny logo centered in a rifle sight, accompanied by the caption "We're going rabbit hunting." The ad went on to read, "If you can catch a rabbit once, you can catch him again. That's what we did in Germany and France. The United States market will be the next to fall. We are going to catch this rabbit in his own backyard. We are the magazine that gives men what they are looking for."

And so began the pornography wars. *Penthouse* declared a full offensive in an attempt to dominate the market. In 1974 Larry Flynt joined the fray, launching *Hustler* magazine. As these publishers pressed to achieve a larger share of the market, they pushed the envelope of acceptability. In a short period of time, the images depicted in these magazines changed from erotica to full frontal nudity. Over the next twenty years, the content of these publications included ever increasingly hardcore depictions of sex.

The technology of the 1970s and 1980s then catapulted pornography into a multibillion-dollar industry. Cable and satellite TV permitted viewers to access pornography from the privacy of their homes. No longer did users risk being seen purchasing a dirty magazine. Behind closed doors, Americans were beginning to do in private what they never would have considered doing in public.

The introduction of VHS tapes and inexpensive videocassette players magnified the problem. In 1978, one hundred hardcore films were released. In 1996, that number climbed to 8,000. In 2002, over 11,000 hardcore films were released, compared with 470 Hollywood features. Hardcore video rentals increased from $75 million annually in 1985 to $490 million in 1992, and to $665 million in 1996.[4] What happened next, though, makes these statistics seem miniscule by comparison.

The introduction of the Internet in the 1990s granted anyone with a personal computer and Internet connection access to pornography twenty-four hours a day, seven days a week. With little to no restrictions, people of all ages now have access to a vast smorgasbord of smut. All it takes is the click of a mouse to view all sorts of images, from the erotic and titillating to the downright bizarre.

An Invitation to Renewal and Restoration

No question about it, an astonishing number of people within the faith community struggle with sexual sin on the Internet. And it is for them, their spouses, and others who want to help them that this book is written. This book, however, is not just about calling attention to a problem. It is about solutions. With inspiration from Scripture and insight from the behavioral sciences, the book presents specific and practical interventions to assist those struggling with sexual sin stemming from the Internet.

The purpose of this book is to liberate people from sexual sin, not only by educating them to the risks and destructive power of cybersexual behavior, but also by providing the tools and strategies essential for life-changing renewal and transformation.

The format of this book is essentially the same for each chapter. Beginning with personal stories based on the experiences of those who sought treatment at the Hope and Healing Institute, each chapter then provides an analysis of the situation as well as encouraging biblical references intended to inspire hope. Most important, readers will find practical strategies designed to help renew and restore a healthy, Christian sexuality. Questions for Reflection and Discussion at the end of each chapter are designed to be used in

The Reality of Internet Pornography

- According to the Internet Filter Review, worldwide pornography revenue in 2006 was $97.06 billion. They estimate that there are 4.2 million pornographic websites, 420 million pornographic web pages, and 68 million daily pornographic search engine requests.
- According to Media Metrix, Internet users view over 15 billion pages of adult content in a single month.
- Child pornography is one of the fastest-growing businesses online, and the content is becoming worse. In 2004, the Internet Watch Foundation found 3,433 child abuse domains; in 2006, they identified 10,656 child abuse domains.
- Worldwide revenue from mobile phone pornography is expected to rise to $1 billion and could grow to three times that number or more within a few years.
- In research conducted by the Polly Klaas Foundation, almost one in eight youth ages eight to eighteen discovered that someone they were communicating with online was an adult pretending to be much younger.
- Forty-two percent of Internet users aged ten to seventeen had seen online pornography in a recent twelve-month span. Of those, 66 percent said they did not want to view the images and had not sought them out.
- Sex is the number-one searched-for topic on the Internet.
- Sixty percent of all website visits are sexual in nature.
- According to *Today's Christian Woman*, one out of every six women, including Christians, struggles with pornography.
- Fifty-one percent of pastors say cyberporn is a possible temptation. Thirty-seven percent say it is a current struggle. Four in ten pastors have visited a porn site.

—Data provided by Enough Is Enough[5]

a small group setting and allow participants to share their own observations, experiences, and insights as they respond together to the material they've read.

Our hope is that you will discover that the solution to recovery is a renewed relationship with God. Throughout these chapters may Christ's gentle call inspire changed thoughts and behaviors and a new way of living.

Sexual struggles are not new. The Bible narrative shows that humanity has struggled with sexual issues throughout the ages. Joseph encountered sexual temptation when Potiphar's wife tried to seduce him (Gen. 39:7-19). Sexual gluttony contributed to the destruction of Sodom and Gomorrah (Gen. 18:16-33). Lot and his two daughters had an incestuous relationship (Gen. 19:30-38). Abraham believed his wife was incapable of conceiving a child, so he chose to have an adulterous relationship with Hagar (Gen. 16:1-16). Believing she was a prostitute, Judah slept with his daughter-in-law (Gen. 38). Sexual manipulation is implied in the story of Samson and Delilah (Judg. 16). King David abused his power in order to have an adulterous affair with Bathsheba (2 Sam. 11-12). David's third son, Absalom, rebelled against his father and had sexual relations with all of his father's wives (2 Sam. 16:21-22).

Warnings against adultery are specified in Proverbs 6:20-29, and the destructiveness of adultery is portrayed in the metaphor of Jerusalem as an adulterous wife (Ezek. 16). In his letter to the church in Rome, the apostle Paul addresses the multiplicity of ways in which people rebel against a covenant relationship with God, including sexual immorality. Similar admonitions appear in Paul's letter to the church in Corinth, one of the largest seaports in the Roman Empire and a city renowned for sexual excesses and immorality. Paul insists that such practices not be tolerated in the church (1 Cor. 5).

The Bible is a book about relationships: about people's relationship with God and with each other. It tells authentic stories of real people, in all their complexity. Like us, our biblical ancestors struggled with temptation. Like us, surrounded by a secular, sexualized culture, they made bad choices.

But the stories in the Bible are also stories about redemption. And so are the stories you are about to read in this book. These are stories of real people from the faith community who have experienced the dark, chaotic forces of cyberspace. As clients who sought treatment at the Hope and Healing Institute, they have agreed to share their stories. Only names and other identifying information have been changed to protect their privacy.

One of their stories may be your story. Our prayer is that, by the grace of God, you too will accept God's invitation to renewal and restoration.

Questions for Reflection and Discussion

1. Do you think online pornography is any more tempting or worse than the "dirty" magazines and pictures people used to use? If so, in what way?

2. How has online pornography affected your life or the life of someone you know and love?

3. What insights does Scripture have for those who are struggling to overcome addiction to pornography and for their families and friends?

Chapter 2

I Was Just Curious

The Temptations of Internet Pornography

Dave's Story

My name is Dave. For about three years, though, I might as well have been known as Dr. Jekyll or Mr. Hyde. I lived a secret life contaminated by pornography.

Nobody knew about my dark side until the week after my wife threw a surprise party to celebrate my fortieth birthday. She had invited practically everyone and anyone we had ever known: family, my parents, friends, the pastor, and even my boss. She and the kids put together a PowerPoint presentation detailing my life's journey. Most of it was humorous, but there were some photographs that served as a stark reminder of who I had been and what I had become.

After the presentation came speeches. My eldest son talked about me being the coach for just about every team sport my kids ever played. He poked fun at me, suggesting that I had wanted to relive my childhood (which was probably true). He talked about me always being at his teacher conferences, and about the time he was in the sixth grade school play and I canceled a business trip just to be there. He mentioned how I was always pestering him and his brother and sister to do their homework and joked about "Dad's alarm clock" that seemed to go off at the same time each night when I would make them go to their rooms to do their homework. Little did he know that I would send them off to their rooms so I could do some "work" of my own on the computer.

My best friend gave a little speech poking fun at my receding hairline. His gift to me was a pair of bifocal reading glasses and some hair dye to cover up the gray. In his speech he talked about how he has never seen me lose my temper (except when the Yankees lost the World Series to the Diamondbacks). He called me a family man and praised my love and devotion to my wife and kids. Later that night, my wife said she thought it was sweet that I began blushing while my friend was speaking. What she didn't know was that the truth of what I'd been doing online made me feel like anything but a devoted husband and father.

My pastor spoke of my commitment to the church and of my willingness to teach Sunday school and open our home for Bible study. It's true that for the past ten years I have volunteered to teach Sunday school, and for years my wife and I hosted numerous Bible studies in our home. But what my pastor didn't know—what no one knew—was that I used the same computer to write material for Sunday school and to surf the web for pornography.

The showering of praise and attention at my fortieth birthday party was more than I could bear. Later that night, after everyone was gone and my wife and I were lying in bed, I prayed and started to cry. I'm not a touchy-feely kind of guy, but that night's experience cut me to the core. I realized I was no longer the person I wanted to be. I realized I was no longer the person my wife wanted me to be. I realized I was no longer the man that Christ called me to be.

It took me a week to muster up the courage to talk to my wife, but I did it. I had to tell her what was going on, and I had to make a radical change to get my life back in order.

I told her that pornography had not always been a problem for me. Back when I was a teenager, as well as in college, I would occasionally look at my friends' *Playboy* magazines, but it was never something I did on a regular basis. I never bought a magazine or rented a video. Until the Internet came along, pornography had never been a problem for me.

My troubles started out of curiosity.

Our family first connected to the Internet in the early 90s. At that time my motivation (and I say this with all sincerity) was good. I wanted my family to benefit from the web. The kids could do research for their homework, and my wife and I could e-mail family and friends any time. It was relatively cheap and fast. Since my parents were aging and struggling with health problems, I could use the Internet to find information on health care. In fact, I could quickly find just about anything I wanted, simply by typing in a few words and clicking the mouse.

To say that my first encounter with Internet pornography was accidental would be a lie. I knew exactly what I was doing. But I didn't know what I was getting myself into. It was late at night, and my wife and kids were in bed asleep. I turned the computer screen to the side, just in case my wife should walk in. I had heard all the talk about Internet porn and was curious to see what it was all about. That night, after connecting to the Internet, I typed in four letters: p-o-r-n. Within moments of hitting "Enter," I had a long list of sites offering an unimaginable array of choices. I hesitated for just a moment—but not longer. I knew I shouldn't do it, but I clicked the mouse. In that moment, my life took an unexpected turn.

What was I doing? I wasn't the kind of person who would go to the store and buy porn. That just seemed wrong. Besides, I'd rather die than be seen going into an adult bookstore. But here I was on the Internet, looking at porn sites. It was so private and secret. No one knew what I was doing, and there was so much to see. As I surfed, I wondered where on earth they found all those attractive women to pose.

That first experience lasted about an hour—until the family dog walked into the room and nudged the back of my chair. I nearly had a heart attack thinking it was my wife or one of the kids. I remember yanking the power cord right out of the wall. In that moment, a wave of shame washed over me. I momentarily came to my senses. What I'd been doing was wrong, and I knew it. I promised myself that I'd never do it again.

But about a month later, the entire scenario was repeated. It was late at night and everyone had gone to bed. I concocted some excuse to tell my wife I had to work on a project for my boss—the first of many lies. This time I locked the door. I knew what I was doing was wrong, and I didn't want to get caught.

What I found online was beyond anything I ever could have imagined—pictures of women posing provocatively and couples together in very explicit scenes. The pictures ranged from erotic to hardcore. There were seemingly millions of pictures of eighteen- and nineteen-year-old girls. On occasion I would stumble upon something really disgusting, like people having sex with animals. But with the click of the mouse, I could quickly exit that site and surf on to something more appealing. It was a kind of pornographic smorgasbord with some really appetizing stuff and some stuff I'd rather pass over. But that is what made the whole experience difficult to resist! I could surf from site to site in search of more tantalizing choices. If I happened upon something unappetizing, I could quickly bypass it. And all the while I'd keep telling myself that at least I wasn't as bad as the guys who chose to look at the illegal and downright bizarre stuff.

In the beginning, I went porn surfing only once in a while. But before long I found myself looking forward to the times I could be alone on the computer. I found myself returning to some of the same sites. Sometimes I explored different sites. It all depended on how much time I had, and my mood at the moment. The whole experience was very arousing and exciting. I found myself making excuses for my behavior. If my wife wasn't "in the mood" or if I'd had a hard day at work, I'd convince myself that it was OK to go online. I realize now that these excuses only served to justify what I was doing. I knew it was wrong. But I was still drawn to it.

Afterward I would feel depressed and ashamed. I was too embarrassed to talk to anyone about what I was doing. How could I tell my pastor? How could I tell my best friend? How could I tell my wife? I was too ashamed to reveal my secret sin, but the guilt was overwhelming. I made countless promises to myself not to do it again. Sometimes I was successful, sometimes not. I could go for days and even weeks without looking. And when I slipped up, I prayed for forgiveness and the strength to change. But the temptation was too difficult to resist.

As time went on, I learned about chatrooms where people would "trade" pictures. The more I e-mailed pictures back and forth with people I didn't know, the more I came to believe that what I was doing wasn't all that bad. How could it be when I would chat with other guys online—other Christian guys—who also found this stuff nearly impossible to resist?

Must be normal, right? Over time I began feeling less guilty and self-conscious about my activity because there seemed to be so many other guys doing the very same thing. I convinced myself that what I was doing wasn't hurting anyone, and that it wasn't affecting me or my family.

But I was wrong.

For starters, it affected my sexual relationship with my wife. Online I would see pictures and video clips of women and couples doing things that I wanted to reenact with my wife. I found myself wanting sex with her more often and getting frustrated that she wasn't responding the way the women did online. Those women seemed like they could never get enough. But my wife seemed satisfied with making love once a week. I started thinking something must be wrong with her. But it was me. My thoughts, my expectations were being warped by what I was seeing online.

My use of porn also affected my relationships with my children. While I never fully abandoned them, I know that I missed out on an awful lot during these past three years. Soon they will be off to college and our nest will be empty. And for the rest of my life I will regret what could have been.

Most importantly, my use of Internet porn affected my relationship with God. I can honestly say that over these past three years I saw a gradual decline in the amount of time I spent in prayer and devotions. Before my addiction escalated, I would go to worship and sing God's praises. But then I became more like a hollow shell—going through the motions, but never fully engaged. I was turning away from God. By failing to resist the temptation, my time, my energy, and my soul were lured away from my Lord.

And it all started out of simple curiosity.

Curiosity *Can* Kill the Cat

Most Christians will admit, even if only to themselves, that sexual temptation confronts them on a daily basis. Living in an overly sexualized society, we are constantly bombarded with erotic and explicit images. Whether through billboard advertising or TV commercials, the swimsuit edition of *Sports Illustrated* or the Victoria's Secret catalogue, we constantly encounter images that capture our visual attention and tempt our souls. What makes these images so difficult to resist is that we are, by God's design, visual creatures. Our bodies are wired to respond emotionally and physically to something attractive.

In early adolescence, boys begin to realize the powerful draw of visual stimulation. Most men can recall sitting in a junior-high classroom, totally captivated by a girl they considered beautiful. It was infatuation, pure and simple, a response to visual stimulation. As young men begin to mature and develop emotionally, the visual attraction becomes coupled with a desire for emotional and relational intimacy resulting in courtships, expressions of love, and covenant vows of marriage. However, at their core, humans are wired to respond to visual stimuli. When exposed to pornography, there is a natural, physiological reaction. A powerful reaction. One that is hard to resist.

Many people struggle with the temptation to use the Internet to look at pornography. In a moment of weakness, some will look out of curiosity. They've heard all the rumors about the abundance of titillating images and think they'll "just take a peek" to check it out. Some may do just that and never repeat the indiscretion. Others, however, find themselves returning to the virtual world of cyberporn again and again. The reality is that nearly 60 percent of all visits to websites are sexual in nature.[1] Twenty-five million Americans visit cybersex sites between one and ten hours per week. Seventy percent of these people keep their behaviors secret.[2]

Those in the porn industry know full and well that their product is hard to resist. More than that, they are keenly aware of just how addictive pornography can be. In fact, their entire marketing strategy is built upon that reality. The porn industry distributes their product for free, confident that after a short while the user will become hooked and then will be willing to pay for the material. It manipulates and preys upon curiosity-seekers and those who succumb to temptation. As of July 2007, a Google search using keywords "free porn" generated 23 million web pages. Yet even with so much free porn, the industry still manages to generate more than $97 billion in worldwide revenues.[3]

Dogs, Pigeons, and Computer Mice

Most of the clients who seek help at the Hope and Healing Institute describe how their problems with Internet pornography began out of curiosity. They insist that they would never consider going into an adult bookstore, but felt safe exploring pornography in the privacy of their homes. With no one to see them and potentially expose and embarrass them, they felt safe to satisfy their curiosity behind closed doors.

Like Dave, most clients tell similar stories of lives spiraling out of control. None of them intended for or even anticipated this consequence. In fact, many of them believed that they were in control. They were "just looking." They were managing their cyberporn use.

But for each person, something happened that forced them to realize that in fact their lives were no longer manageable. Whether it was a spouse's discovery of their porn use, a child stumbling upon their shameful secret on the home computer, or disciplinary action by an employer for violating the company's Internet-use policy, something happened that made them realize they had a big problem on their hands.

Risk Factors

Three key factors influence sexual expression and interaction on the Internet. Known as the Triple-A Model (developed by Al Cooper, clinical director at the San Jose Marital and Sexuality Center)[4], these conditions make people vulnerable to the powerful temptation to use the Internet to view pornography or engage in other cybersexual behavior:

- **Accessibility.** Pornography and cybersexual material are available twenty-four hours a day, seven days a week. You don't even need to leave the comfort of your home to use it.
- **Affordability.** More than 23 million pornography sites are available free of charge. No credit card. No debit card. No contracts. No obligation. It's all free—until a sexual addiction compels the user to take out the Visa card.
- **Anonymity.** From the privacy of their home or office, those who surf the Internet for sexual material believe they're doing it anonymously. They log on to the Internet using screen names that cloak their identities. People enter virtual reality believing it's a vast masquerade ball.

What had begun as simple curiosity had morphed into something far more sinister and problematic. The changes these people experienced were the result of a psychological phenomenon known as *conditioning*.

Anyone who's ever owned a cat or a dog knows the fundamental principle of conditioning, which was studied and documented by Russian scientist Ivan Pavlov. Pavlov conditioned his dogs to salivate whenever they heard a bell ring. He did this simply by ringing a bell any time he fed his dogs. Before long, the dogs began to salivate when they heard the sound of the bell because they associated that sound with food. The mere ringing of the bell, even with no food in sight, was enough to get the dogs aroused.

Something similar happens to those who use their computers to access pornography. They begin to associate the computer—whether it's the sound of the modem, the gentle hum of the fan, or clicks on the keyboard—with sexual arousal. Curiosity-seekers are unaware that their minds and bodies are being conditioned to associate the computer with pleasurable feelings of sexual stimulation. The result is that their capacity to resist temptation erodes, placing them at risk of developing personal or relational problems, even cybersexual addiction.

Warning Signs

The following are warning signs that a person's use of the Internet has progressed from a momentary spiritual lapse (curiosity) to a something far more problematic:

- **Change in sleep habits.** In a desire to avoid being "caught in the act," those using their computers to access pornography will do so only when they have privacy. In the context of marriage or family, such time can be limited. As a result, those whose curiosity becomes habit-forming will deliberately alter their sleep habits. Some will complain of insomnia. Others will claim a need to "get some work done on the computer" and come to bed later or rise earlier in the morning.

- **Moodiness and irritability.** Although pornography can be physically stimulating, arousing, and pleasurable, most Christians who've fallen to the temptation of pornography are well aware that their behavior is unacceptable. This inner conflict often manifests itself in moodiness and irritability. When struggling with the burden of sexual temptation, those who are typically lighthearted and jovial can appear depressed and often develop a rather short fuse.

- **Demand for privacy.** As curiosity becomes a habit, some will move the computer to a more private location, perhaps in a room with a lock on the door. They may rearrange the furniture so the computer screen is not visible by others in the room. Often they will become easily irritated when interrupted while on the computer.
- **Disregarding other responsibilities.** Some people can become so absorbed in their online activities that they no longer tend to household chores or other family activities. Time once spent cleaning the kitchen or doing yard work, or attending a child's school or sports events, is exchanged for time spent surfing porn sites. Interest in hobbies and other recreational pursuits seems to diminish while time at the computer escalates.
- **Change in sexual appetite.** The sexual stimulation experienced in "virtual reality" causes changes in real-life sexual relationships. For some, this may be manifest in an increased libido or sex drive, or in a change in the types of sexual activity desired. Others may withdraw and seem less interested in sexual contact. Having released sexual energy while online, little is left for "real" sex with their marriage partner.

While Pavlov worked with dogs to demonstrate the principle of conditioning, another scientist worked with birds. Psychologist B.F. Skinner developed what came to be known as the "Skinner Box," a device he used to study the behavior of pigeons.

To condition his pigeons, Dr. Skinner placed his pigeons in a box equipped with a disk upon which the pigeon had to peck in order to get a pellet of food. By trial and error, the pigeons quickly learned that pecking on the disk delivered a pellet of food. So well trained were Skinner's pigeons that they were able to learn the exact number of pecks required to get the desired pellet. Some pigeons were required to peck five times on the disk, others ten or fifty times. Skinner's birds learned that if they pecked they would get what they wanted: food.

Toward the end of Skinner's work, he started running out of pigeon food. This caused great consternation among the pigeons. Their behavior, though, demonstrated the power and drive of a conditioned behavior. Even without the reinforcement of food pellets, the birds pecked continuously, apparently believing the reward would be imminent.

Poor pigeons.

Poor cyberporn user.

Dr. Tom Grundner, author of the *The Skinner Box Effect*[5], demonstrates that a person's behavior can become conditioned by Internet pornography. Like pigeons that receive the reinforcement of a food pellet by pecking, humans experience a reward by viewing material that is sexually provocative and arousing. With every click of the mouse, the person is conditioned to expect more and more. In Grunder's words, computers with Internet access are nothing more than "high-tech Skinner boxes."

There's a big difference, though, between human beings who use a computer mouse to surf for porn and Pavlov's dogs or Skinner's pigeons. Eventually, the dogs got enough to eat and stopped salivating. The pigeons got their fill of pellets and stopped pecking. The human appetite for the rewards of cybersexual stimulation, however, is different. It changes over time.

With every click of the mouse, a person believes that the next image will be more stimulating than the one before. It may or may not be, but the individual keeps clicking anyway. In time, the sexual appetite becomes insatiable. The person begins to desire something more—more provocative, more stimulating, more exciting. The process continues until the person finds the "perfect" image that causes climax through masturbation.

Just as dogs and pigeons have their appetites satisfied when fed, users of Internet pornography believe that their sexual appetites are satisfied after a session of surfing results in orgasm. This, however, is a false perception. It's the reason why so many people who access pornography out of curiosity put themselves at risk of greater problems. Although orgasm signals the end of the event, their appetites continue to grow and change.

In the initial stages of exploring the world of Internet pornography, it does not take much to achieve stimulation and arousal. Over time, however, people discover that to achieve the same level of arousal or experience the same euphoric feeling, they must either spend more time with the material or seek images that are progressively more stimulating. The issue is tolerance. Just as someone who is developing a drinking problem begins to notice that it takes more alcohol to experience the same effect as before, so a user of Internet pornography discovers the need for more or "stronger" images.

In the early stages, erotic images of scantily clad people are enough to achieve the desired effect. But as the appetite for pornography changes, the person begins looking for images of people engaged in particular sex acts, or ventures into chatrooms, or seeks out the novelty of video downloads or live two-way interaction. Others may find their curiosity (now a conditioned response) leading them to explore interaction with increasingly younger persons or to view bizarre or perhaps illegal material.

Those who venture into the virtual world of pornography, then, put themselves at risk that the psychological phenomenon known as conditioning will actually shape their sexual appetite.

Graham Crackers, Corn Flakes, and Sexual Self-Control

Health food and diet plans are nothing new. About 150 years before the South Beach Diet or the low-carb craze, a gentleman by the name of Sylvester Graham pioneered America's first health food crusade. His concern was not for cholesterol or weight management. Instead Graham (the inventor of the Graham cracker) advocated the consumption of bland foods and the elimination of meat from one's diet, believing that spicy foods contributed to erotic thoughts and sexual excesses—among them masturbation and sexual intercourse more often than once a month.

There were also others who linked the ideas of nutrition and sexual self-control. Health food advocate James Caleb Jackson invented America's first cold cereal, made from something similar to crushed graham crackers. He called his product "granola." A few years later, John Harvey Kellogg, nutritionist and campaigner against the "dangers" of masturbation, introduced a food known as corn flakes. Like Graham's crackers and Jackson's granola, Kellogg's bland concoction was intended to curb one's sexual appetite.

Although crackers and cold cereals have never proven effective at curbing sexual thoughts or behavior, the single goal that led to their invention was the need for sexual self-control.

As the apostle Paul suggests, "Do you not know that your bodies are temples of the Holy Spirit, who is in you, whom you have received from God?" (1 Cor. 6:19). Our bodies are to be treated as temples. They are to be tended as places where God is worshiped and glorified. Anything we bring into a temple that dishonors God is a desecration.

Graham and Kellogg weren't so far from the mark when they campaigned against diets that included too much spice. They simply focused on the wrong appetite. Consumption of pornography does contribute to sexual excess. And, since it has no redeeming value, nor does it in any way honor God, it should be eliminated from the diet.

Scriptural Guidance for Dealing with Temptation

> At that time Jesus came from Nazareth in Galilee and was baptized by John in the Jordan. Just as Jesus was coming up out of the water, he saw heaven being torn open and the Spirit descending on him like a dove. And a voice came from heaven: "You are my Son, whom I love; with you I am well pleased."
>
> At once the Spirit sent him out into the wilderness, and he was in the wilderness forty days, being tempted by Satan. He was with the wild animals, and angels attended him.
>
> —Mark 1:9-13

Christians know that evil exists—and not just because the Bible says so. We know it because we experience it. It's impossible to pick up a newspaper or turn on the news and not recognize that there are powerful destructive forces at work in our world. Those who are acquainted with the world of Internet pornography and cybersex can offer testimony that the Prince of Darkness is real, alive, and flourishing. They can give testimony because they have suffered from or struggled with pornography. For them, the story of Jesus' wilderness experience provides great hope. This passage is the story of how Jesus wrestled with Satan in the wilderness for forty days and emerged victorious from that experience.

In Mark's account of Jesus' baptism and temptation, note how quickly the author transitions from one scene to the next. In one sentence God declares his love for Jesus, and in the very next sentence the Spirit "sent" him into the wilderness to be tempted by Satan. The Revised Standard Version says that the Spirit "drove" Jesus out into the wilderness. In one moment Jesus celebrates his divine calling, and in the very next his mission is put to the test. In one moment a voice from heaven ordains Jesus' ministry, and in the very next he is sent into the wilderness to test his resolve to resist temptation and to fulfill his calling to his divine mission.

In the faith community we believe that God has called us to follow Jesus. We may not literally hear a voice speak from heaven, but we experience it nonetheless in our hearts. On Sunday mornings as we worship, we celebrate our calling as Christians. But come Monday morning, we face temptations— temptations that may distract us from our true calling as Christ's disciples.

In the wilderness Jesus was tempted. The other gospel accounts of Jesus' wilderness experience describe these as very real temptations, like hunger, that are a natural part of being human. Jesus was tempted to turn stones into loaves of bread so that he could appease his hunger. There is nothing evil about hunger. Our bodies exert energy, and that energy must be replenished by rest and nourishment. Similarly, there is nothing evil about sexual desire. Like hunger, desire is a natural consequence of being human.

So how did Jesus resist the temptation to satisfy his need for hunger? And what would that mean for those who struggle with the temptation to satisfy sexual urges outside of the context of a marriage relationship?

The story of Jesus' wilderness experience shows that Jesus kept his focus on God. Faced with real and powerful temptations to satisfy his own needs, he chose instead to focus on the reality that God had called him to serve a greater purpose.

He dealt with temptation by believing that God would not abandon him.

As people called by God to be followers of Jesus Christ, we are not exempt from the temptations Jesus himself experienced. Jesus withstood the agony of temptation by never losing sight of his mission and ministry. For forty days Satan tempted Jesus in the wilderness, and for forty days he discovered the power that helped him keep his focus on the truth—that no matter what Satan used to tempt him, God would be with him. Like Jesus, we too have the assurance that even in our own the wilderness experiences, God will not abandon us.

No matter how stimulating or arousing or appealing our temptation may be, God is with us. No matter how destructive the dark forces of chaos may be, God does not leave us. No matter how much we fear that our curiosity may have gotten out of control, God still believes in us.

Just as the gospel text says, God provides angels to minister to us in our wilderness. If we dare to disclose our struggle to fellow believers, God will use them to minister to us. And just as God fortified and strengthened Jesus for his ordeal in the wilderness, so too God will fortify and strengthen us. When the forces of evil inundate us with sexual temptation to the point where we risk being defeated, strength is available to us through God's network of messengers. We just need to muster the courage to ask for their help.

The faith community recognizes and understands the reality that evil exists in the world and attempts to damage our relationship with God. We can be tempted and led astray if we are not watchful and careful. To tempt us to use pornography, Satan gains a foothold through our curiosity. Of course, curiosity—to wonder about the world and all that goes on within it—is in itself normal. But it can also be the first step to giving into temptation. People who are "just curious" about pornography may begin a process of escalation: they want to explore "a little more" or "a little longer." And before they realize it, their curiosity has become a habit.

A letter written by James, one of Jesus' brothers, offers this practical perspective:

> Blessed are those who persevere under trial, because when they have stood the test, they will receive the crown of life that God has promised to those who love him.
>
> When tempted, no one should say, "God is tempting me." For God cannot be tempted by evil, nor does he tempt anyone; but each of you is tempted when you are dragged away by your own evil desire and enticed. Then, after desire has conceived, it gives birth to sin; and sin, when it is full-grown, gives birth to death.

> —James 1:12-15

Evil is a very real presence in our world. And unless Christians have a specific strategy to resist sexual temptation, they put themselves in jeopardy of being "dragged away" by their own desire. Yes, sexual desire is a God-given gift. But those who use pornography to stimulate that desire are at risk of developing unhealthy sexual desire.

Healthy sexual desire is found in the context of a loving, caring marital relationship. Pornography, on the other hand, tempts people to explore that desire outside of the covenant relationship of marriage. When people see images of sexually attractive people engaged in intensely provocative activities, their sexual desire is activated or triggered and, if not controlled, can lead to fantasies that contribute to even more unhealthy sexual thoughts. Because their sexual fantasies are no longer focused on their marriage partner, their sexual desire is reduced to nothing more than lust.

It's essential, then, that Christians challenge themselves to control their sexual desires. Failure to do so puts them at risk of embarking on a progression of sexual sin. The initial stage of the cycle is pleasurable. When humans first encounter pornography, there is an immediate biological reaction. Within milliseconds of viewing something sensual and provocative, the mind is flooded with sensory messages that convey the message that what is being looked at is good. Pornographic images have a powerful, magnetic force, drawing the person to look—even as he or she recognizes the sinfulness of the material. Suddenly, the person is confronted with a battle between impulse and self-control. If in weakness someone begins using pornography, his or her spiritual resistance begins to erode, especially if the experience is reinforced by masturbation.

For Christians who are well aware of the sinfulness of pornography and yet choose nonetheless to use it, justification of the behavior is the next natural step. In order to feel good about themselves, they have to rationalize the behavior, and this only reinforces the cycle. Typically, as the desire for sexual sin increases, the justifications for such behavior get more elaborate. Justification minimizes the feelings of shame and guilt, which are meant to alert us that our attitudes, perceptions, and behaviors may be morally wrong.

With pornography so readily available on the Internet, Christians are faced with a very real threat to their souls. Like Dave, many Christians will be tempted. Some will resist the powerful grip of pornography, while others will become captive to it.

Strategies for Dealing with Temptation

Take Action Now
Sexual self-control is about more than abstaining from the use of pornography It is about managing sexual desires and behaviors. Christians should develop an action plan to manage the powerful temptation of pornography. To resist

the temptation toward cybersexual sin, we recommend you do the following:

- **Get rid of the computer.** While this may not be an option for many people, others may have to ask themselves if they really need to have a computer in their home. In an age where computer terminals are available at most public libraries, you may need to consider living without one.

- **Change your Internet service provider.** Many service providers, such as America Online and Comcast, provide uncensored access to the Internet. Although these are excellent service providers, the unmonitored access may be too problematic. You may want to consider service providers that censor objectionable material.

- **Install protective software.** Many software programs are available that screen and filter pornography. This is strongly recommended, especially for those who have children with access to the computer. Filtering products such as Net Nanny and Cybersitter are good resources but have limitations (primarily the need to know a porn site's address on the Internet) that prevent them from keeping up with the pace of new sites being added to the Internet each day, allowing some porn content to get through to your screen.

- **Put the computer in a public place.** It may not fit with your décor, but the lack of privacy in your living room will discourage the temptation to use the computer to find pornography.

- **Limit computer time.** Covenant with yourself and with your spouse to limit the amount of time you spend on the computer. Agree to not use the computer while alone, if possible. Instead of spending hours on the Internet, try spending one hour a day while other family members are around. If you find it difficult to follow this rule, maybe the computer has become a problem.

- **Delete previously saved material.** Those who download pornographic images are tempted to keep a collection of material. Keeping this material only makes it easier to relapse and repeat the behavior you are trying to control. Permanently delete it.

- **Do something else.** Find something else to do with the time you spend using the computer to access pornography. Whether it's volunteering at a soup kitchen, stamp collecting, or fly-tying, your thoughts and energy need to be focused elsewhere.

- **Ask yourself why.** Understanding why you use pornography may actually help you resist the temptation to do so. If you use pornography because you feel lonely, you need to focus on developing friendships. If you think pornography helps reduce tension, you need to find other ways to manage your stress. If you use porn because something's missing in your marriage, you need to attempt to resolve the problem rather than compound it.

- **Not convinced it's a problem?** If you feel that your use of pornography is mere recreational fun, and not a problem, we suggest that you give it up for a while. Decide to refrain from using it for a specific time period—say three months. If you aren't able to stay away from pornography for that period of time, maybe you do have a problem after all.

Accountability

Secrecy is Satan's tool. The prince of darkness uses secrecy to undermine our resistance to temptation.

Most Christians use pornography in secret. While they would be too embarrassed to be seen at an adult bookstore, they choose the apparent anonymity of the Internet to access

A Pastor's Perspective

People need two things in life: to be held and to be held responsible for their actions.

It takes courage for someone like Dave to admit his problem. It also takes courage for members of a congregation to hold each other accountable, especially because of the shame and guilt that comes with sexual sin. Accountability can feel like judgment and rejection. So it's important to address the reality of temptation in the context of Christ's unconditional love. Our criticism and discipline must focus on what the person has done and not the character of the person who did it.

More than anything else, our goal is to hold each other up as children of God—to believe that the same power that breathed into us the breath of life is present with us when we are faithful and when we succumb to temptation.

pornography. A driving force that perpetuates this behavior is secrecy. In not wanting their shameful behavior to be exposed, they will go to great lengths to erase the history and delete their computer's temporary Internet files. And as they work diligently to avoid being caught, Satan celebrates their gradual spiritual and relational decline. Secrecy gives Satan great satisfaction as people grow more and more distant in their relationships with their spouses and their relationships with their God.

A key to resisting temptation, therefore, is revealing the secret. Muster up the courage to admit it. Allow yourself to be held accountable by others, in addition to your spouse. Make connections with other Christians who similarly seek to protect themselves. Arrange for regular meetings or contacts with a peer group at your church, or connect with a trusted friend. Knowing that you have to tell someone else about your actions can provide powerful motivation to resist temptation.

Journaling

Keeping track of circumstances that may weaken your resistance is one method for successfully resisting temptation. We recommend that you keep a small, pocket-sized notebook with you at all times for approximately four weeks. This is not a "Dear Diary" type of journal. Rather it's a place to record events that make you feel sexually tempted throughout the day. Write down the time, the circumstances immediately before the event, your mood, a brief description of the event (content, duration, and the like), and your thoughts afterward. At the end of each day, spend a few minutes reviewing your entries. Most likely, you'll notice a pattern. You may discover, for example, that the temptation is greater at certain times of the day. Or it may be influenced more by mood, or factors within your marriage, or circumstances at work. Realizing these patterns will help you learn what areas of your life require change.

Some people use journaling as a therapeutic tool, writing their sexual autobiography. In fact, many of the vignettes included in this book are excerpts from the autobiographies of clients at The Hope and Healing Institute, written as part of the therapeutic process. By writing their stories, they became better able to reflect on their lives and, in so doing, became more aware of their strengths and coping skills. By writing your own sexual history, you too can identify factors that put you at risk of succumbing to sexual temptation.

A Word from Dave

Fortunately, I have been able to get my behavior back under control. By the grace of God, I made a decision to tell my wife about my struggles. Together we spoke to our pastor, who put me in contact with a small group of men whose stories are similar to mine. Like messengers from heaven, these men have ministered to me in a way I never imagined. They have helped me to be honest with myself. They have helped me to be accountable. They have helped me become a more spiritually mature, more disciplined follower and servant of Jesus Christ.

Questions for Reflection and Discussion

1. What do you think about the reality of Satan? Is Satan found outside us or within us?

2. What tools or resources do we have for dealing with sexual temptation? What works for you?

3. What does it mean to you that Jesus was tempted?

Chapter 3

Can You Handle the Truth?

Confrontation and Confession

Jan and Steve's Story

I'm middle-aged, my boobs are beginning to sag, and I have hemorrhoids. To be sure, I wasn't feeling too good about myself. I used to be fairly confident about myself, but my self-esteem began to swirl down the drain when I discovered that my husband was using porn. How was I supposed to compete?

I've known Steve for more than twenty-five years. We were high school sweethearts. We've raised four children, three of whom are now in college. Our youngest son is finishing his senior year in high school. It's always been our dream to make sure all our kids would go to college, and then we'd settle a bit and take some time for ourselves.

Our marriage had been good for the most part. Like most marriages, we've had our ups and downs. I'm not sure there is such a thing as a perfect marriage. We've had our share of financial struggles, but I think we've done well for ourselves. When the kids were younger I was a stay-at-home mom and Steve worked very hard to build his business. Once the kids hit high school, though, I found a job. We needed the money, and with the expense of college tuition for all three of our kids, we knew we'd have to tighten our budget. We weren't wealthy, but we were able to make ends meet. Life was moving along in a good way. I was happy for the most part, beginning to dream of what life would be like for us as "empty nesters."

My dreams, though, never involved the problems we were about to encounter. Never in my worst nightmare did I ever imagine that my husband had a problem with pornography.

It was about five years ago when we switched our Internet service provider from a telephone modem to high-speed cable. I was surprised that Steve was willing to pay the extra expense, but the kids were doing so much online research for their homework assignments that it seemed reasonable. Not long after, though, we started getting e-mails advertising porn sites. I asked Steve about it, and he told me not to worry about it. But I was worried. Worried about my kids. Frankly, I never gave much thought to worrying about Steve.

Being a good, protective mom, I watched the computer history to monitor what my kids were up to. One day I discovered that the computer had been used to go to some porn sites. The record indicated that it happened at a time when the girls were at a church retreat and our son was at a basketball game. I was hurt and angry. I didn't know how to confront Steve. I guess I was afraid I would find out that after all these years he found me less attractive than he used to. It took me a good week to muster up the courage to talk with Steve, and when I did, the conversation lasted no more than five minutes. He actually apologized for not telling me that he "accidentally" went to a site, not knowing that it was a porn site. He said he tried to click out of it as soon as he realized what it was. He said he didn't tell me because he was concerned that I would be upset.

And I wasn't upset. Not then. But over the next five years we have had this same conversation no less than half a dozen times. And each time he would become more and more angry, accusing me of being paranoid and overly suspicious. And each time I confronted him I'd come away wondering if I was the one with the problem.

But a few months ago I crawled off to bed early. It was a Friday night and I'd had an exhausting week. A few hours later I woke to discover that Steve had not yet come to bed. I glanced at the clock. It was one o'clock. Steve is usually in bed by eleven. I figured he had fallen asleep on the couch. He's done that before and woken up with back pain—and in a bad mood. To save myself the grief of living with a grump, I went downstairs to get him to come to bed.

I discovered Steve sitting at the computer looking at pornography. I gasped. He was startled and quickly turned off the computer monitor. No words were exchanged between us. I went back upstairs, took his pillows and tossed them on the floor outside our bedroom door. He could sleep on the floor, for all I cared.

I didn't sleep a wink. I don't think I've ever been that upset.

The next morning I got up, not certain of what would be said or done. I made some coffee. I didn't know what else to do. When Steve came into the kitchen, I asked him if he wanted some coffee. It just seemed like the right thing to do. We sat at the kitchen table in silence for the longest time. I saw the pain in his face, and I'm sure he saw the pain in mine. I finally found the courage to speak. (Maybe God had given me the right words at this time, because I couldn't do all this by myself.) I told Steve I wanted to know everything. The truth. The whole story.

Steve told me that for the past five years he'd been battling with a desire to use pornography—and losing. After all these years, after all the times I'd confronted him, he finally confessed that what I suspected was actually true. It was a surreal moment. Although blazing with anger that he had lied to me on so many occasions, I was relieved to finally get the truth.

Steve told me that for him, porn was like a drug. Over time he wanted to do it more and more. The more he looked, the more he wanted. It started out of curiosity, he said, but within weeks he looked at it whenever he was at home alone. It didn't take long though, and he would do it when I was in the shower and the kids were downstairs watching TV. He admitted that sometimes he would masturbate while looking at pictures. This was very difficult for me to listen to, but I knew by the shamed look on his face that it took a lot of courage for him to disclose this.

As he talked, I kept trying to tell myself that this was *his* problem, not mine. But to be honest, I really felt that this was about me. I know I don't look the same as I did when we were first married. I felt sad that maybe he didn't feel attracted to me anymore. And I felt angry that I had to compete with the women in the porn pictures he was looking at. Steve tried to tell me that this wasn't about me, but that is exactly how I felt.

I told him I had a thousand questions. I told him I expected to hear the truth. He told me that he would be honest, but asked if we could do something first before I started asking him questions.

He asked if we could pray.

It had been years since we had done that. And in that moment I knew things were going to be all right. We asked God for guidance to sort through this. We asked for strength to keep our marriage together. We asked God to help us understand what went wrong.

It has taken a lot of time to sort out all the feelings and confusion. I'm still really angry about pornography. It has touched my family in a deadly way. Sometimes I still have feelings of rejection and hurt, and when he is home alone, I wonder if he is looking at pornography again. I think this is all very normal. It takes time to rebuild trust once trust has been shaken. But I have confidence that Steve will win this battle, and I will do my best to be supportive. He knows he has hurt me, but he's trying hard to make up for this. I told him that the best gift he could give me was to simply leave pornography alone, once and for all, and make a recommitment to live a Christ-oriented life.

Do You Want the Truth?

Do you want to know the truth? Do you want to know the truth about your partner, yourself, and your marriage? Can you handle it? Do you have the courage to confront it? Is your partner willing to confess the truth? That is, of course, the purpose of confrontation: to expose the truth so something can be done to right the wrong.

Of course, Christian couples face the same kinds of challenges as nonbelievers. Our faith does not make us immune to temptation or shield us from problems associated with lust. Even though they may be fully aware that cyberporn is a major problem in society, many Christians are reluctant to face the truth that their own lives, their own marriages are at risk. Most people in the Christian community find it difficult to imagine that their spouses could be surfing the Internet for pornography. They consider the person they married to be, for the most part, loving, loyal, kind, and considerate. But users of pornography? It just doesn't seem to fit with the type of person they thought they'd married.

Many people who later discover that their husband or wife struggles with pornography will tell you that although they suspected that something was wrong, they never imagined that cyberporn was the culprit. They just could not fathom the idea that the person with whom they worship on Sunday could surf porn sites come Monday morning. They may sense that something just isn't right, but they don't know exactly what it is. They have no major marital problems or issues, but they're aware of an emotional distancing in the relationship.

Strange as it may seem, many Christians consider their cybersexual behavior to have little effect on their lives, including their marriage. They may view their experiences with cyberporn as merely recreational. Just for fun. Even though their spiritual foundation makes them fully aware that their behavior reflects a measure of spiritual weakness, pornography is difficult to resist. The problem, however, is more than temptation—it's also perception. Those who engage in cybersex often fail to see how problematic or damaging pornography can be.

What began as mere curiosity can quickly escalate to become a cancer-like force that has the power to erode a loving, covenant relationship. A couple is at greatest risk when they fail to heed the warning signs of a problem. Porn users need to correct their perception and see that their "recreational" use of pornography is causing changes within themselves and is damaging their marriage. Spouses need to realize the risks of sexual temptation available on the Internet.

Anticipate Denial

If you suspect that your husband or wife may be struggling with Internet pornography, you (as his or her spiritual partner) must be courageous enough to confront your partner. The word "confrontation" itself has negative connotations, suggesting bitterness, anger, and resentment. But from a Christian perspective, confrontation is an act of accountability that embraces your spouse in love for the purpose of encouraging him or her to be the person God intends.

When confronted with the reality that life has been polluted by cyberporn, a natural reaction is that of denial. It is important, however, to keep in mind that denial is not simply a make-believe, Pollyanna-ish attempt to pretend that something is not happening. In the field of psychology, denial is considered a defense mechanism, and as such, it serves a purpose. In the case of confronting cybersexual behavior, the most obvious purpose is self-protection. When confronted with the truth about themselves, people experience a range of emotions, including embarrassment, guilt, and fear. Most users of cyberporn believe that their activity on the Internet has been anonymous. Not much consideration is given to the possibility of discovery. When confronted, however, the individual experiences a wave of embarrassment and guilt. And just as a swimmer in the ocean braces himself when confronted with a powerful wave of water, so your spouse may brace himself with an initial response of denial. In many ways this is normal. Anticipate denial. It allows the person time (whether a few seconds, hours, or days) to admit what is really going on.

The best way to manage denial is to challenge it with information. Communicate your concerns and observations. Talk to your spouse about what you have noticed; for example, becoming more irritable or coming to bed later than usual. You are not accusing; instead you are communicating an observation and wondering if anything is going on. Of course, you must leave open the possibility that your spouse may minimize these things or provide alternative explanations. If you suspect, however, that the problem is associated with pornography, you need to be prepared to present evidence to help your spouse move beyond denial.

To prepare for a healthy, productive confrontation, your first task is to become computer literate. Even in a culture in which everything seems to be dependent on computers, it is not unusual for people to possess limited knowledge on how computers operate. If you suspect that someone is struggling with a cybersexual problem, it is important for you to develop your knowledge of computers.

We suggest that you learn some basics about checking the Internet history, website "cookies," and temporary Internet files. As you do so, remember that the intention is not to prove your spouse's guilt. On the contrary, the intention is to gather information so that you can lovingly challenge the denial and help your spouse move beyond shame and guilt toward change and renewal. Before you proceed to gather this information, therefore, we strongly encourage you to ask God to keep your intention focused on problem-solving rather than fault-finding.

If you have a computer that operates on a Windows operating system, there are two easy methods for checking the computer history:

- Access the web browser (for example, click on the icon for AOL, Firefox, or Internet Explorer). On the tool bar, click the History button. The History bar appears, containing links for websites and pages visited in previous days and weeks. In the History bar, click a week or day, click a website folder to display individual pages, and then click the page icon to display the web page. To sort or search the History bar, click the arrow next to the View button at the top of the History bar.

- Click on the Start button and scroll up until you find the Control Panel. You can also access this area by clicking on the "My Computer" icon on the computer screen. Click on the Control Panel icon, and a dialogue box will open, offering access to Network and Internet, from which you can access "Internet Options." In this dialogue box, select "Settings" from the Browsing History section. By clicking "View Files," you will then see a list of "Temporary Internet Files." Notice that there are buttons that also delete these files as well as Internet cookies. Click on "View Files" and a list will appear. These are files that attach to your computer whenever you visit a web page on the Internet. By scrolling down the list you will be able to discern if any of these sites are pornographic. Be prepared, however, because some of the language associated with these file names is rather graphic and vulgar. Notice also that the information available also indicates the date and time the material was accessed. You may also discover that the information in these files has been deleted. This may cause you concern or alarm if you think it represents a deliberate attempt to hide the computer's history. Be aware, however, that these files do take up disk space and may have been deleted deliberately not for the purpose of "covering tracks" but to open up space on the computer's hard drive.

If you have an Apple/Macintosh system you can check the history in this way:

- First, open your Safari browser by clicking on the Safari icon in the dock. Click on History in your Safari menu, located at the top of your screen. When the drop-down menu appears, the most recent history (the last ten web pages visited) will appear.

- Directly below it you will find the rest of the recorded browsing history, grouped by day into sub-menus. If more than ten web pages have been visited on the current day, there will also be a sub-menu present labeled "Earlier Today" containing the rest of today's history.

Even if your spouse denies responsibility for the information you discovered on the computer, you have still accomplished a great deal in helping draw attention to a potential problem. Even if he or she has chosen to not admit a potential problem, you have communicated that you have the know-how to check the computer's history. This may contribute to any hesitancy that your spouse may have to access Internet pornography.

There is the possibility, however, that he or she may become more diligent to erase the history in an attempt to "cover up." We recommend, therefore, that in your initial conversation you covenant with him that no one, except you or another accountability partner, will delete this computer information. This is a simple way for your spouse to demonstrate to you that he or she has not succumbed to temptation.

Consider Motivations

If you have gathered information that your spouse uses the computer to access pornography or engages in some other form of cybersexual behavior, it is helpful to take time to consider possible motivations for doing so. While the impulse may be to immediately confront the problem, we strongly encourage you to prayerfully consider why. Poor preparation and a premature confrontation may result in even more emotional distance between you and your spouse.

Is it recreational?

It sounds offensive, but the reality is that many use their computers to access pornography as a form of recreation.

A Note About Monitoring Software

Out of concern that there is a problem, some people purchase computer software that records the activity conducted on a home computer. In some cases this software is loaded onto the computer in "stealth" mode—that is, the people using the computer may not be aware that their activity is being monitored. We discourage the use of such products, at least during the initial stages of confrontation. Clinical experience indicates that those who chose such an approach often find the confrontation sidetracked away from the original intention. The typical response is a complaint of a breach of privacy, and the conversation becomes convoluted as the person defends his or her own trustworthiness. We recommend instead that you gather information in regard to history, cookies, and temporary Internet files, as described above. Keep the conversation focused on the problem and on how to develop a strategy toward positive change.

For them the sexual act is entirely mechanical. There is no emotional attachment to the persons depicted in the images and the experience is completely devoid of relational intimacy. Most women, however, find it difficult to understand the disconnect between sexual intimacy and emotional intimacy. If your spouse's use of porn "means nothing" to him, then communicate to him what it means for you. As partners in a covenant relationship, you are bound to honor one another, and if pornography jeopardizes this, then it must be jettisoned from the relationship.

Is it a problem in the marriage?

Some say they turn to the computer for pornography because they feel a sense of sexual neglect. Hearing this, many spouses become angry, feeling as if the blame is projected onto them. For many couples, therefore, the process of confrontation is quickly derailed as they attempt to affix blame on each other.

In order to keep the process of confrontation and confession productive, couples need to recognize that the use of pornography may represent and reflect a failure of marital communication. Not the wife's failure. Not the husband's failure. But a failure of marital communication. Use of pornography may be symptomatic of a problem within the marriage. Some couples have unspoken sexual issues that date back to the early days of their marriage, but they have learned to avoid addressing them. Solving the problem, therefore, requires a willingness to address the issues.

In a sense, Christian marriage, albeit a covenant partnership, is fundamentally a selfish enterprise. That is to say, two people are in relationship because they need each other. For multiple reasons, you need your spouse to be in your life, and your spouse also needs you. When each of you feel as if your needs are met, you feel good about yourselves and each other. But the moment one of you feels that your needs are being neglected, there is a break in the harmonious relationship and the relationship is put at risk. In healthy relationships, couples are able to communicate their sense of dissatisfaction and negotiate changes so that both persons feel satisfied. A healthy relationship involves a collaborative effort at satisfying each other's needs.

When it comes to sex, a healthy marriage needs to be mutually satisfying. But many couples find it difficult to talk about sex. Even when a couple has joined together in the intimacy of sex, they may nonetheless feel awkward talking about the subject. As a result, many couples fail to address issues of frequency, initiation, and the various types of sexual activities that they enjoy. The failure to communicate may lead to resentment, and the consequential sense of neglect may contribute to a decision to use pornography.

For couples in which the behavior of one person is associated with a disturbance in the sexual relationship, the key for remedy is to develop communication skills and reach collaborative agreement so that both partners feel sexually satisfied.

Could it be something else?

Prior to any confrontation, it is essential to consider other explanations for the behavior. This is not to minimize the problem, but to suggest that the behavior may reflect some other psychological phenomenon. For that reason, we strongly encourage that individuals struggling with issues related to pornography consult with a mental health professional to determine if the use of pornography is symptomatic of a more extensive problem.

Some people who suffer from depression look for ways to self-medicate. More than feeling "blue," depressed people agonize with painful emotions. Some turn to alcohol, others to drugs as they seek to find ways to soothe the pain. Some discover their "medication" in Internet pornography. Why? Because it is visual material that elicits a physiological response. Any human being who has ever been sexual recognizes that sexual activity creates pleasurable physiological changes. There is no need to drink alcohol or ingest drugs. The human body can create its own chemical change by becoming sexually aroused and stimulated. For persons who are experiencing a mood disorder, this causes a temporary alleviation of the depression. The fix, however, is temporary. As with alcohol and drugs, it actually compounds the depression. Although the chemical "high" during the sexual experience seems to provide relief, the sense of shame and regret afterward contributes to an even more profound depression. Some persons, seeking relief again from the agony of depression, repeat the cycle time and time again, continuing the downward spiral of depression.

Others experience what is called a "bipolar" depression. This mood disorder is punctuated not only with periods of depression but also with moments of heightened energy. In the field of mental health, these periods are referred to as "manic" or "hypomanic" episodes. During these times, some bipolar persons become uncharacteristically more talkative while others attend to chores or other activities like the Energizer bunny. For some, this energy is expressed sexually. More than an active libido, the person's sex drive is kicked into overdrive. Their partners feel as if they "can't keep up." Unlike a person with a normal sex drive, persons experiencing a hypomanic/manic episode sense that they can't get enough or feel as if their sexual appetite is insatiable. For a bipolar person, therefore, heightened sexual activity (including excessive pursuit of pornography) is reflective of a hypomanic or manic episode.

Obsessive Compulsive Disorder is one of the most common mental disorders. Research indicates that 6.5 million people struggle with OCD, an anxiety disorder that involves recurrent obsessions or compulsions.[1] Obsessions are intrusive thoughts, impulses, or images. Some people who suffer from OCD have recurrent worrisome thoughts that they may have forgotten to turn off the coffee pot or lock the door. Throughout the day their thoughts are focused and concentrated on the overwhelming worry that their home may burn down or be burglarized. Compulsions are behaviors that a person feels compelled to perform in order to diffuse the compulsive thoughts, such as returning home to check the coffee pot or verify that the door has been locked. While on the surface this may seem anything but problematic—maybe even practical—a person with OCD would return home on multiple occasions, experiencing the same anxious thoughts time after time. For some people, the obsessions involve thoughts of sex. Such people experience intrusive thoughts about sex and sexual interaction without provocation. It's as if the thoughts become trapped in their minds. They obsess on these thoughts and find relief only by acting on the impulse. Some experts believe that cybersexual behavior is a symptom of this disorder.

Scriptural Guidance for Confrontation and Confession

One evening David got up from his bed and walked around on the roof of the palace. From the roof he saw a woman bathing. The woman was very beautiful, and David sent someone to find out about her. The man said, "She is Bathsheba, the daughter of Eliam and the wife of Uriah the Hittite." Then David sent messengers to get her. She came to him, and he slept with her. (Now she was purifying herself from her monthly uncleanness.) Then she went back home. The woman conceived and sent word to David, saying, "I am pregnant."

In the morning David wrote a letter to Joab and sent it with Uriah. In it he wrote, "Put Uriah out in front where the fighting is fiercest. Then withdraw from him so he will be struck down and die.

So while Joab had the city under siege, he put Uriah at a place where he knew the strongest defenders were. When the men of the city came out and fought against Joab, some of the men in David's army fell; moreover, Uriah the Hittite died.

The Lord sent Nathan to David. When he came to him, he said, "There were two men in a certain town, one rich and the other poor. The rich man had a very large number of sheep and cattle, but the poor man had nothing except one little ewe lamb he had bought. He raised it, and it grew up with him and his children. It shared his food, drank from his cup and even slept in his arms. It was like a daughter to him.

"Now a traveler came to the rich man, but the rich man refrained from taking one of his own sheep or cattle to prepare a meal for the traveler who had come to him. Instead, he took the ewe lamb that belonged to the poor man and prepared it for the one who had come to him."

David burned with anger against the man and said to Nathan, "As surely as the Lord lives, the man who did this must die! He must pay for that lamb four times over, because he did such a thing and had no pity."

Then Nathan said to David, "You are the man!"

—2 Samuel 11:2-5, 14-15, 16-17; 12:1–7a

Sooner or later, those who regularly use pornography are confronted with the realization that their cybersexual behavior is out of control. And when confronted, they have a choice: denial and rationalization or facing the truth. Even though they are well aware of what they are doing, users often convince themselves that their activities have been done in complete secrecy and anonymity. They have been able to protect their secret from exposure, believing that what they do behind closed doors is unknown and undetectable. And when confronted, they are forced to shift their thinking. Confrontation means that either they maintain the charade of secrecy or they recognize that their sin has been exposed and the jig is up.

Those who have ever had a problem with pornography are familiar with rationalization. A phrase that echoes in their thoughts over and over again begins with the words, "At least I'm not . . ."

"At least I'm not having a real affair." "At least I'm not looking at kiddy porn." "At least I'm not pressuring my wife to do things she doesn't want to do." "At least I'm not paying for it; I'm only looking at free stuff." "At least I'm not doing it when my kids are around." "At least I'm not into really kinky and perverted stuff." "At least I'm not a letch around other women." "At least I'm not at the strip clubs or adult bookstores." "At least I'm not meaning it when I cyber with those people."

People who use pornography often enter the valley of the shadow of self-deception. That is what happened with David. David was in the valley of the shadow of self-deception when God sent the prophet Nathan to get him turned around. Nathan told David about a poor man who had only one sheep that he had raised as a family pet. The poor man's children had played with the sheep, and the animal had been fed from their table. One day, their neighbor, a rich man with large flocks, took the poor man's one sheep and killed it, serving it to a visitor.

As a former shepherd, King David was indignant. He was incensed. He demanded to know the rich man's name so that he could be punished. Nathan said simply, "You are the man."

It was the moment of truth.

In that instant a surge of shame must have welled up within David. A lump in his throat. A knot in his stomach. Faced with the truth, this was a moment for decision.

No doubt about it, David had a choice. Nathan had no authority over him. David was the king. He knew he could dance around Nathan's accusation. He had the power and the authority and finesse to dodge the bullet of truth. But in that moment of confrontation, David made a decision to become radically committed to moral purity. In that moment of truth, David was able to face his shame, the shame of realizing what he had done. Had he only taken a sheep from Uriah, David could have restored it a hundredfold. But he could not give back a life that he had destroyed. He could not give back a life he had taken away. He could not undo the past. There was no rewind button.

Sooner or later the truth will be exposed. Maybe when Human Resources calls to inform you that you have been fired for violating the company's Internet use policy. Maybe when your child stumbles upon something you downloaded but forgot to delete. Maybe when you find yourself arranging for a real-life meeting with someone you have met in cyberspace. Maybe when the knock at the door is not a UPS delivery but an FBI agent. Or maybe when your partner asks, "Honey, how is it with you? Has it been a problem?" Maybe it will happen when you get to Nathan's line "You are the man" in the story of David and you realize that God is talking to you.

What do you do when confronted with the truth? You have a choice. You can continue to deceive yourself, deceive your partner. Or you can do what David and Bathsheba did: face the consequences. What happened to David and Bathsheba?

Their first child died. It is inconceivable that God would cause the death of an infant because of his father's sin, so this story does not suggest that those who are guilty of sexual sin will be punished in such a way. But there will be consequences. As Scripture tells us, the wages of sin is death.

For individuals or couples struggling with cybersexual sin, something has to die. Old patterns of denial, patterns of self-deception, patterns of rationalization, all have to die. Are you afraid that maybe your marriage won't be able to survive if you disclose your struggle? There is no guarantee it will, but as Christians you have been given faith to trust in the power of resurrection. Before there is resurrection there must be death. That might mean that certain aspects of that old relationship, old expectations, and old ways of relating have to die.

When faced with the truth, when faced with his shame, David accepted the consequences. And when he heard about the child's death, he got up, took a bath, covered his body with lotions, put on clean clothes, and went to pray in the house of the Lord. He came back again and ate, and then went in to comfort Bathsheba. Do not miss the powerful symbolism of what he did when he decided to be radically committed to moral purity. By accepting the truth about himself, there was no need to continue living a life of self-deception. He was washed clean, forgiven. He worshiped God, who made it possible. He nourished himself spiritually and physically, and he pledged his love and support to Bathsheba.

Years later David wrote a psalm that has special meaning for those who have walked in the shadows of shame and self-deception:

The LORD is my shepherd, I lack nothing.

He makes me lie down in green pastures,
he leads me beside quiet waters,

he refreshes my soul.
He guides me along the right paths
for his name's sake.

Even though I walk
through the darkest valley,
I will fear no evil,
for you are with me;
your rod and your staff,
they comfort me.

You prepare a table before me
in the presence of my enemies.
You anoint my head with oil;
my cup overflows.

Surely your goodness and love will follow me
all the days of my life,
and I will dwell in the house of the LORD forever.

—Psalm 23

As Christians we believe in the power of resurrection. We believe there is hope not only for the sinner, but also for those who have been sinned against. By the power of resurrection there is a second chance not only for those who go on living, but also for those whose lives have been destroyed by sin. We believe that the resurrection means that someday the tangled web we have created will be straightened out. Righteousness will be restored, and we will dwell in the house of the Lord forever.

Strategies for Confrontation and Confession

The purpose of any confrontation is to discern and determine the truth. The truth, however, can be difficult to face. We suggest that you take the opportunity to pray, seeking God's guidance and wisdom as you prepare to encounter the truth. Prayer will help you develop the appropriate tone for the conversation. Prayer will allow you to confront with supportive understanding and confess with resolute honesty. Prayer will help you prepare for what you may learn and discover in the process of confrontation. You are, after all, afraid of what you may find. You are concerned about your spouse's reaction. You may fear your own reaction. You may struggle with embarrassment over having to talk about sex and sexuality. Take the opportunity to contemplate these things and present them to God in prayer. Use your own words or those of the suggested prayers that follow.

A Wife's Prayer

Gracious God, you know how nervous I am. I know something is bothering my husband, and part of me does not want to face what it may be. I think I know what it is, but I am so afraid. Afraid of what I might discover about him; afraid of what this might mean about me. I'm so afraid.

But I do trust you, O God, and so I pray for your blessing upon us in this difficult time. You blessed us on our wedding day when we promised to love each other for better or for worse, in sickness and in health. But this is not the kind of sick I anticipated, O God. I am sick in heart and wounded in spirit. You, O God, have blessed us throughout our marriage, and I trust in your continued blessings as we try to work through this. You brought us together and you have blessed us with a good history. I pray that our history will be a strong foundation to help us withstand this current storm.

I need your help, Lord. Help us be strong enough to talk about this without anger and hostility. Help me to communicate my feelings while at the same time trying to understand his struggle. Help me to listen in a supportive way and to choose my words carefully. Help me not to be judgmental but to encourage him to be the man you intend him to be. Amen.

Setting the Stage

Before committing yourself to the process of confrontation and confession, you'll need to invest much time and energy into preparing what to say. This will set the tone for healing to begin. Couples need to be cautious, however, in recognizing that "speaking" is only a fraction of the communication process. So in addition to preparing what you want to say, you'll need to prepare yourself to listen.

If you are praying for God's Spirit to guide you through a productive exchange of confrontation and confession, you may find inspiration in the story of Pentecost in the Book of Acts. When the Holy Spirit came upon those gathered in Jerusalem, a miracle happened:

Suddenly a sound like the blowing of a violent wind came from heaven and filled the whole house where they were sitting. They saw what seemed to be tongues of fire that separated and came to rest on each of them. All of them were filled with the Holy Spirit and began to speak in other tongues as the Spirit enabled them.

Now there were staying in Jerusalem God-fearing Jews from every nation under heaven. When they heard this sound, a crowd came together in bewilderment, because each one heard their own language being spoken.

—Acts 2:2-6

Countless blessings were experienced that day, not the least of which was the gift of hearing. Though different languages were being spoken, the power of the Holy Spirit enabled them to hear and understand what was being said. And so, as you prayerfully prepare for confrontation and confession, you need to do more than anticipate your own words or tone. You need to focus attention on how well you will listen to each other.

Consider Tone, Timing, and Terrain

Pay attention to the manner in which the prophet Nathan approached King David. He was well aware of David's transgressions, but in confronting him, Nathan elected to use a metaphor designed to provoke a sympathetic response. David, once a shepherd boy himself, was indignant at the story of a man who slaughtered a family pet. The prophet put the conversation in an emotional context, approaching this emotionally charged and potentially volatile subject in such a way that David would be prepared to recognize his sin.

We encourage you to approach your spouse in a manner that elicits more honesty and less defensiveness. Of course you do not have control over the response, but you can work carefully to set the stage for a productive conversation. The first consideration is tone. It may seem silly, but practice out loud what you intend to say. Practicing will enable you to discover that even though you are avoiding language that is harsh and judgmental, you may still be communicating judgment through your tone. You may want to consult with a friend who can provide helpful feedback or use a tape recorder. With practice you can work toward developing a tone that resonates both concern and a determination to get to the truth.

A second consideration is timing. When do you and your partner communicate best? In the morning at breakfast or in the evening after the kids are in bed? On a weekday or on the weekend? By reflecting on your relational history, you may recognize a pattern to your communication style and discover that some times are more conducive for communication than others.

Terrain is another factor to consider. Where do you and your spouse communicate best? Reflecting on your history can help you recognize that you communicate better in some places than in others. If, for example, you have a history of arguing in the bedroom, you will want to avoid confronting your spouse in that room. Find the best place to talk, whether it's in the kitchen, on the deck, or in the car.

Practical Communication Skills

It is estimated that the average rate of speech is 125 words per minute. The average person, though, can think four times faster, at 500 words per minute. A person's brain can begin formulating a response even as it is receiving verbal information. In many cases this means that people are listening with only about 25 percent efficiency, actually hearing only one out of every four words. And when the conversation is complicated by heightened emotion (anger, hurt, or frustration), there is a substantial decrease in listening comprehension.

For many couples, communication skills are similar to driving skills. When an individual first learns to drive, there is intense focus and concentration on the many factors involved with operating a potential death machine. The driver pays attention to speed, traffic patterns, blind spots, and lane changes. Later, after the driver has developed some experience, some of that focus and the attention begin to slip away. Driving becomes routine. It's not unusual for experienced drivers to drive their vehicle from point A to point B and, upon arrival, realize that their thoughts were so preoccupied with something else that they wonder how they ever made the journey.

Something similar occurs with relationships. Early on, couples focus intense attention on communication patterns, carefully crafting the spoken word and attentively listening to what is being said. Over the course of time, though, the couple becomes more comfortable, and listening skills may slip into autopilot.

Actually hearing only one out of four words, the listening partner's brain (in autopilot mode) filters through what they "think" is being communicated. Capturing only every few words, the listener quickly determines whether what is being said is important or interesting. The level of engagement in the conversation is reduced to radar, scanning the speaker's comments for "hot-button" words that the brain has identified as exceptionally meaningful. Just as the phrase "free food" might instantly capture the attention of a hungry teenage boy, there are certain vocabulary words in marriage relationships to which the brain is exceptionally sensitive.

Conversations that are focused on something as volatile as the use of pornography and cybersex typically include certain words and phrases, such as "hate," "disgust," "sickening," "gross," and "angry." But when the listener is only capturing one out of four words, and is filtering only the potentially threatening words, there is potential for the conversation to be disastrous.

Developing certain key skills can help couples become more effective and productive in their ability to communicate when confronting problems associated with cybersexual behavior. These skills include the following:

Body Language

Face your partner squarely. Close proximity is best, conveying the message that this is a relationship problem and that you are willing to confront this together. Be cautious what you do with your posture. Don't cross your arms. You want to convey a willingness to receive a response and avoid the nonverbal communication of judgment. In addition, maintain good eye contact. You are not only looking at your partner's face, you are looking into his or her heart and soul.

Paraphrase

Paraphrasing is an essential skill in that it gives you an opportunity to determine whether you have accurately heard what your partner has attempted to communicate. It is a process in which you restate in your own words the content of what you hear the other person say. Note that this is not mimicking or parroting verbatim. Rather it is mirroring and rephrasing the other's words so that you both know you fully understand what has been spoken. It is also gives your partner a chance to correct you if you have misinterpreted the comments, or to rephrase what he or she intended to communicate.

Paraphrasing is a very time-intensive task, and many couples fail to invest enough energy in clarifying what is being said and heard. Unfortunately, most marital communication breaks down at the onset of a conversation either because of a failure to paraphrase or an inaccurate interpretation of what has been communicated.

An example of a derailed conversation might sound like this:

Wife: I'm concerned about how much time you have been spending on the computer lately. With so many men struggling with pornography I wonder how it's been with you.

Husband: So you think I'm a pervert?

From the get-go, this conversation has been derailed. The husband failed to paraphrase and has become angry (and possibly defensive). In order to prevent this conversation from escalating into an argument, the wife needs to rephrase her initial comment and ask her husband to paraphrase. By deliberately slowing the pace of the conversation and working cautiously to be certain that communication is accurately presented and received, there is a greater likelihood of a productive outcome. In this case, the husband could paraphrase by saying, "You're concerned about how much time I've been spending on the computer. And you worry that I might be looking at pornography. Am I right?"

Both husband and wife have a responsibility to clarify what has been communicated in both nonverbal and verbal communication. In the example above, the husband may comment, "The tone of your voice seems a little judgmental, and I can't help but feel a little defensive."

Couples should understand that the skill of paraphrasing must be used throughout any conversation wherein clear communication is essential. It is not isolated to only the first few comments, but continues throughout the conversation, even to the point of resolution.

Perception Check

This communication skill involves seeking to clarify what you think you "see" happening. In a sense you are guessing what is going on, because you truly do not know. All you know is what you see, and what you see may not be interpreted accurately. For example, in a conversation in which you are confronting your spouse about his use of pornography, you may observe him rubbing his forehead. Based on visual observation, you might conclude that he is angry with you. But your perception may not be accurate. You truly do not know exactly what he is feeling. And so you need to ask. In a nonjudgmental manner, you state your observation and offer an interpretation of what it might be—and then ask for clarification. For example, you might say, "I see you rubbing your forehead. I'm wondering if you are angry with me. Am I right?" Of course your intuition may be correct, but it also may be wrong. He may instead be rubbing his forehead out of utter shame and embarrassment. If the conversation had continued with you believing that he was angry, the direction of the conversation may have taken a turn for the worse.

A key component to the perception check is admitting that your perception may or may not be accurate. You need to be able to communicate your perception without presuming that it is accurate. The words you use are exceptionally important. The most effective perception checks begin with phrases such as, "I get the impression that . . ." "It seems to me that . . ." "I'm wondering if . . ." "It sounds to me as if . . ." "Is it possible that . . ." "I get the feeling that . . ."

After stating your observations, be sure to ask a question so that your partner knows you realize that your perception may be inaccurate. Effective perception checks are followed with questions such as, "Am I right?" "Is that correct?" "Is this how you feel?" "Is that true for you?" Keep in mind there is no way for you to know with absolute certainty what the other person is thinking or feeling. You need to ask.

Time Out

When a conversation involves heightened emotion, one of the most beneficial interventions couples can use is a "time out." At any point in the conversation, either party has the right to request a time out, at which point the conversation comes to an end. Especially when the conversation becomes unproductive, calling a time out is an effective way to bring the conversation to temporary closure. But the key is "temporary." Whether the person requests five minutes, thirty minutes, several hours, or a day, the intention is to keep the conversation productive. It is not a way to get in the last word or to cut your partner off from saying something you do not want to hear. Neither should it be a time to step away from the conversation in order to regroup and develop a new strategy for "winning" the argument. If that is the intention, the time out is nothing less than manipulation. Rather, the purpose of a time out is to allow each person time to focus attention on resolving the issue at hand.

The person requesting a time out must be specific about how much time is being requested. For example, you could say, "I need a time out. Let's take five minutes (or an hour or a day)." After that time is up, the person who made the request must reinitiate the conversation. A couple can take as many time outs as needed. When used with respect for each other, couples can use this technique as a primary tool for transforming potentially hostile arguments into productive, solution-focused conversations.

A Word from Steve

Dear Jan,

I don't know if you realize it, but today is an anniversary of sorts. It was exactly a year ago that you discovered me ut tho computer. It was the worst day of my life. But in a strange way, it was also the best. I will never, ever forget the disappointment on your face when you walked in on me. And I will never forget your courage to force me to face up to what I was doing to myself (and to you). For too long I was too afraid to face up to the truth about myself. And you, my sweet bride, had the courage to confront my problem.

When I look back at the changes in our marriage in this past year, I can't help but feel glad for the changes we have made. Our communication is better (way better) and I feel as if I understand you and you understand me like never before.

Thank you, Jan. For everything.

Love, Steve

Questions for Reflection and Discussion

1. The text from 2 Samuel says that King David made a private confession of his sexual sin in the temple. But later he wrote Psalm 51, which was to be read publicly. What are the risks of public disclosure of sin?

2. What are the possible benefits to confessing sexual temptations and sins to others?

3. Is the church a safe place to confess sexual sin? Explain.

4. How well is your church prepared to understand and hold accountable those who struggle with sexual temptation? How should the church respond if pastors or other leaders are found to struggle with pornography?

Chapter 4

Can You Forgive Me?

Forgiveness and Reconciliation

Kathy and Tom's Story

I had long suspected that Tom was using the computer to look at pornography, but every time I confronted him he assured me that nothing was going on and that I was just being paranoid and distrusting. On one occasion I checked the computer history and discovered that he had gone to some pornographic website. When I asked him about it, he told me that some guy from the office had sent him something as a joke. He acted as if he was deeply offended and morally outraged that his friend would do such a thing. He said he didn't want to tell me because he didn't want me to be upset.

That is what he said, but deep in my heart I knew it wasn't true.

He lied to me.

I know this because I walked in on him and saw for myself exactly what he was doing. He was sitting there at the computer looking at an incredibly graphic picture. And he was masturbating.

It was bad enough to have walked in on him, but his reaction made me hurt even more. He suggested that I was overreacting. He said things like, "It didn't mean anything," "I didn't mean to hurt you," "This wasn't about you, it was about me," "It doesn't mean I don't love you, or want you," and "It doesn't mean anything is wrong with 'us.'"

All I could do was stand there and cry.

He slept on the couch that night. The next day we didn't talk about it. Actually, we didn't talk about it for days. Days of silence between us. I wanted to know what was going on with him, but I was afraid to ask. Maybe I was afraid of the answer.

After several frustrating days, Tom finally broke the silence. He came home early from work and told me he had a confession to make. He told me he had a problem with looking at pornography on the computer. He said he wanted to stop, but it was like he couldn't help himself. He said he didn't mean for this to ever be a problem, but over time, he became more consumed with it.

He asked me to forgive him.

Of course I said yes. It is what I was supposed to do. He said he was sorry. I could see the regret and remorse on his face. There was sadness in his eyes. What else was I supposed to say?

But that didn't make the pain and confusion go away.

Over the next few months, I struggled with trying to understand Tom's desire for pornography. I wanted to be supportive of him, but I couldn't help but feel angry, sad, and resentful. I was angry at Tom and at our culture that seems so preoccupied with sex. I was sad that something might be wrong with our marriage; sad that he might not find me attractive anymore. And even though Tom finally admitted he had a problem, I still resented that he had lied to me all those times.

I tried to talk to Tom about how I felt, but it was as if my feelings fell on deaf ears. He would have a glazed-over look in his eyes, like he was looking at me but not listening. Over and over he would tell me that he was sorry but didn't know what else to say. And so after a while he said nothing at all, telling me that I had to get over it.

It made me wonder if he even cared. It was depressing. I cried myself to sleep many nights. I knew he heard me. Why didn't he do or say anything? Why not just touch me on the shoulder and let me know everything would all be OK? Just say or do something!

I wish he would understand what this has been like for me.

Doesn't he care that I lay awake at night worrying if our marriage will survive? Doesn't he notice that I have felt so sick over this that I am hardly eating? Does he realize that this is about me too?

Despite Tom's reassurances that he would not look at pornography again, the trust has been broken. I said I forgave him, but I wonder if I really ever did. My feelings were a mixture of guilt and anger: guilt that I couldn't seem to forget what he had done; anger because it seems so unfair that I even have to deal with something that I'm not responsible for.

He asked me to forgive him and I said I did. But why can't I forget? Why can't I get over this?

Cybersex: A Breach of Fidelity

"I didn't mean to hurt you."

"This wasn't about you, it was about me."

"It doesn't mean I don't love you, or want you."

"It doesn't mean anything is wrong with 'us.'"

These are typical reactions from porn users offering assurance to their spouses that their cybersexual behavior has had minimal effect on their marriage. These sorts of comments are not surprising, since most people who use cyberporn actually believe that their behavior has little to no negative effect on their lives or relationships. But these comments stem from a perception wherein they consider the use of pornography to be "recreational." Their partners' perception, however, is radically different. They consider the use of pornography to be a breach of trust in the marital relationship.

In an online survey posted on the MSNBC website over a seven-week period in 2000, 9,265 people admitted to using the computer to view pornography or engage in cybersex. Participants in this extensive research study responded to two questions examining how pursuing online sexual materials may have interfered with or jeopardized certain aspects of their lives. Overall, 32 percent of the entire sample identified at least one area of their personal life that has been negatively affected by their online sexual pursuits. Twenty-one percent of all respondents reported that their online activities had jeopardized an area of their life. Interference was most reported in their personal life, and the most common area of life jeopardized by online sexual pursuits was relationships.[1]

72

While the MSNBC study suggests that the majority of cybersex participants did not experience negative effects, another research study focused on the wives and partners. In this study, conducted by Dr. Jennifer Schneider, 100 percent of respondents experienced serious adverse consequences of their partner's cybersex involvement.[2] Her research determined that cybersexual behavior has profound effects on intimate relationships, including the following:

- Issues of trust and decreased intimacy were key factors in relationship problems.

- Being lied to repeatedly was a major cause of relational discord.

- Cybersex was a major contributing factor to separation and divorce.

- Two-thirds of couples experienced a serious decline in sexual relations as a result of one partner's cybersex involvement.

- Sixty-eight percent of couples lost interest in relational sex.

- Over 50 percent of those who turned to the virtual world to explore pornography and sex showed a decreased interest in sex with their real-life partner.

- Thirty-four percent of the partners were less interested in sexual intimacy knowing that their significant other was engaged in online sexual activity.

- As a consequence of cybersex, some couples had had no relational sex in months or years.

Dr. Schneider also explored the effect of a parent's cybersexual behavior on children. Her research documented that the primary effects on children include the following:

- Increased chance of exposure to computer-based pornography.

- Involvement in parental conflicts.

- Lack of attention because of one parent's involvement with the computer and the other parent's preoccupation with the cybersex addict.

- Breakup of the marriage.

The Importance of Validation

When there has been a break in the relationship due to cyberporn or cybersex, the offending spouse must come to terms with the effect of the behavior on his or her partner. The person needs to understand that when a spouse becomes aware of what has been going on, he or she experiences a vast array of emotions, including feelings of hurt, abandonment, betrayal, rejection, loneliness, shame, humiliation, jealousy, anger, and loss of self-esteem. These are very real feelings that deserve validation. When these feelings are dismissed or minimized by the offending spouse, suggesting that the person is overreacting, it only adds insult to injury.

When encountering their partner's use of Internet pornography, people experience a variety of thoughts and feelings. Common reactions include the following:

- "I don't really know what emotion to feel right now. I'm just numb all over."

- "I don't know if I should cry, get mad, yell, or hit him."

- "What did I do wrong? Maybe this is all my fault."

- "Should I leave him? Kick him out? Make him sleep on the sofa? I'm so confused, I don't know what to do or who to turn to right now."

- "Should I tell my parents? Should the kids know what's going on?"

- "I'm scared. I feel like my world is falling apart."

- "How could she do this to me? I thought we had a good marriage."

- "How can I compete with all those young women? My butt is bigger, my breasts are sagging, and I've given birth to children. I'm not twenty anymore!"

- "What else he is hiding or what else has he done? I'm afraid there's another secret he hasn't told me about."

- "I don't know if I can ever forgive her. This hurts so deeply."

- "Maybe I can forgive him over time, but I'll never forget."

- "I thought we had a good sex life. What am I doing wrong?"

- "Does she love me anymore?"

- "Why couldn't he come to me and tell me about this problem?"

- "Have the kids seen any of these pictures on the computer? I'm afraid to ask them."

- "I feel like a victim. I've done nothing wrong to deserve this."

- "Why did God let this happen to my marriage?"

It takes time to understand and sort out all these thoughts and feelings. For some people, it can take years to cope with something that is so emotionally painful and traumatic. For others, the process can move along more quickly. Each person is unique; each moves along at his or her own pace. It's important for people to know they are not alone; that their thoughts and feelings are similar to those of others who have experienced their spouse's cyber-infidelity. And it is critically important for their spouses to understand fully the depth of pain their partners are experiencing because of their choice to use Internet pornography.

A Break in the Covenant Relationship

The covenant relationship of marriage involves emotional and sexual loyalty. At the marriage altar, Christian couples enter a relationship pledging vows of fidelity and unconditional love. But what is a couple to do when the vow of loyalty has been breached as one partner strays into the world of cyberporn and cybersex? Although the person may consider the behavior to be meaningless and devoid of emotional intimacy, their partner is more likely to consider the behavior to be a bona fide form of infidelity. Even though there has been no "real" contact, spouses consider their partner's online sexual experience to be just as emotionally painful as real affairs. The sad reality is that not all Christian marriages can survive the emotional turmoil associated with cyberporn. In fact, online sexual activity is increasingly cited as reason for divorce.[3]

Christian couples, therefore, are faced with a dilemma. There has been a breach of fidelity, but there has also been a pledge to love one another without condition. In commitment to that covenant vow, couples should attempt to work through the often-difficult process of forgiveness and reconciliation. Not all couples, however, are capable of accomplishing this process. If you are in an abusive, hostile relationship, we strongly encourage you seek pastoral guidance and counsel.

For some couples, the rupture in the relationship is one painful moment of discovery. Perhaps the wife discovers something on the computer or actually walks in and catches her husband in the act. Immediately there is a confrontation and the process of healing begins. For other couples, the breach of promises has occurred on multiple occasions. Perhaps many times there was the suspicion that something was wrong, but when asked, their spouses offered excuses rather than confession. Or a spouse hears a promise not to repeat the transgression, only to discover later that the pledge has been broken again.

Many times husbands or wives have heard words of regret and promises to change, only to discover a continued pattern of betrayal.

Whether the transgression has been confronted immediately or over the course of time, couples face the difficult task of engaging in the process of forgiveness and reconciliation. But although this process is the hallmark of the Christian tradition, many in the faith community have never received training or specific guidance on how to accomplish genuine forgiveness and reconciliation.

Some common misconceptions about forgiveness compromise many couples' capacity to achieve reconciliation.[4] These misconceptions include the following:

- **Forgiveness means forgetting.** Not only is this impossible, but to forget may actually perpetuate the problem. Whenever there has been a violation in the marriage contract, the result will be some measure of pain. To forget is to pretend that the pain was never there. The reality is that the initial injury leaves an emotional scar. That scar, unfortunate as it may be, serves as a reminder not to repeat the hurtful act.

- **Forgiveness means no consequences.** For a marriage partner to offer amnesty (that is, to drop the charges, requiring no penalty, recourse, or punishment) is to take away from the wrongdoer the necessity of showing penance. For reconciliation to be complete, the wrongdoer must have an opportunity to demonstrate, by words and actions, a sense of regret and a desire to offer restitution.

- **Forgiveness is an event.** In fact, true forgiveness and reconciliation is a process that requires an enormous investment of emotional and spiritual energy, and it is not likely to be accomplished in a brief period of time. The process is time-consuming, although there is no set, prescribed period of time. What some couples may be able to accomplish in a few hours may take others weeks or months to achieve. The issue is not so much the amount of time, but whether both partners are actively working toward forgiveness and reconciliation.

The Process of Forgiveness

In a book on forgiveness entitled *Forgive and Forget*, award-winning author Lewis Smedes discusses the importance of moving from hurt and hatred to healing and reconciliation. He describes how forgiveness is not an event but a process. He emphasizes that we cannot expect to win spiritual and emotional battles instantly. Just as we do not expect a widow to accept her husband's death immediately without grieving, so we cannot expect victims to forgive the wrongdoer immediately. The cycle of forgiveness, like the cycle of grief, must run its course before reconciliation can happen.

For Those Who Have Been Wronged

For those who have been wronged, betrayed, or violated, there are (according to Lew Smedes[5]) four identifiable steps in the process of forgiveness:

- **Recognize and admit that there is pain.** When your spouse causes you pain, don't pretend you don't suffer. Don't pretend the wrong doesn't matter. It does matter. Your partner has chosen to set his or her eyes on someone other than you, and this action has cut you to the core.

- **Recognize the hate.** Recognize the human instinct that when a person hurts you, you want the offender to suffer as much as you have. You may not hate your spouse, but you hate what the person has done. But be careful; hate (like radioactive nuclear waste) can destroy you. It saps the soul, leaving it weaker than before, too weak to create a better life beyond the pain.

- **Recognize that there is healing.** You cannot change the past, but you can heal the hurt that comes to you from the past. In this step, you recognize that the power source for healing comes from outside yourself. You recognize that when Christ commands us to forgive, when he commands us to love our enemies, he also gives us the power to forgive, the power to love.

- **Recognize that there is reconciliation.** There will come a time when you invite the offender back into your life. Because you will never forget the initial offense, life will never be the same. By the grace of God, your lives together could possibly be even better than before.

For Those Who Have Done Wrong

For those who have violated the relationship by indulging in pornography, there are four levels in the process of repentance (the peak of which is reconciliation):

- **Perception.** This step stresses the importance of understanding the unfairness of what you did. No, you don't have to understand everything. You probably will never understand fully how hurt your partner is. No matter. Accept the verdict. Admit that what you did was thoughtless and selfish.

- **Pain.** At this second level of repentance, you feel the pain that you inflicted. At the first step you articulated words. Now it is time to demonstrate that those words have meaning. Allow yourself to have these feelings, even if it feels bad. Try not to deny or block out your feelings. It is important for your spouse to know you feel bad about what you have done.

- **Confession.** To confess, in a spiritual sense, is not merely to admit that you did something wrong. To confess is to enter the heart of the one you hurt and to tell this person that you hurt as he or she hurts. When you confess, you stand naked in the eyes of the one you hurt, pleading nothing but the hope of grace. This is the most difficult step. It is almost unbearable. For it is harder sometimes to confess to another human than it is to confess to God.

- **Promise.** This is the last step in the process of repentance, the step that allows reconciliation to occur. Once you have come to understand the wrongness of what you did, once you have revealed your feelings to the one you offended, you have a passionate desire not to hurt that person again. You want to be trusted again, and you are ready commit to that person that you will be worthy of trust. Expressing the desire to change creates hope that change will occur.

A Pastor's Perspective

Kathy said that she cried herself to sleep for many nights after Tom confessed his problem with online pornography. We tend to be more comfortable with tears when the pain is raw; when we first experience the reality of our wounds. But as the process of reconciliation proceeds, some mistakenly believe that tears should dissipate.

For Kathy, tears continued to percolate to the surface weeks and months after Tom confessed. But those tears do not necessarily represent the harboring of resentment. They may instead be a welcome reflection that the process of reconciliation is working

What are tears, after all? Tears cleanse debris from our eyes. Tears cleanse debris from our souls. These cleansing tears are a reminder of the waters of baptism, which symbolize what it means to be forgiven and to forgive.

Scripture Guidance for Forgiveness and Reconciliation

Some time later, Jesus went up to Jerusalem for one of the Jewish festivals. Now there is in Jerusalem near the Sheep Gate a pool, which in Aramaic is called Bethesda and which is surrounded by five covered colonnades. Here a great number of disabled people used to lie—the blind, the lame, the paralyzed. One who was there had been an invalid for thirty-eight years. When Jesus saw him lying there and learned that he had been in this condition for a long time, he asked him, Do you want to get well?

"Sir," the invalid replied, "I have no one to help me into the pool when the water is stirred. While I am trying to get in, someone else goes down ahead of me."

Then Jesus said to him, "Get up! Pick up your mat and walk." At once the man was cured; he picked up his mat and walked.

—John 5:1-9

Do you want to get well? Do you want your marriage to get better? Do you want to work through the process of forgiveness and reconciliation?

This story from the gospel of John offers spiritual wisdom to those who turn to Jesus for healing. It takes place at the pool of Bethesda. The gospel writer calls all the people gathered there "disabled" and makes specific reference to them as blind, lame, or paralyzed. Among this group was one individual in particular who had been sick for thirty-eight years. He and the others were at the pool for a purpose. It was not just a place for disabled persons to congregate. Rather it was a place where people looked for the Spirit of God to heal them.

This pool was located near the Sheep Gate on the northern side of the Jerusalem Temple. People believed that on occasion an angel of the Lord stirred the waters in the pool, and the first person to step in after the angel had come would be healed. We can imagine that day after day, year after year, this individual would sit near the pool—waiting for the waters to be stirred by the healing power of God. And time and time again, others would reach the pool before him when the waters were stirred.

Clearly this man hoped to be healed. He believed that God had the power to heal him. He only lacked the ability to enter the pool when the waters were stirred.

Jesus approached this person and asked, "Do you want to get well?"

He responded by pointing out to Jesus the predicament he was in: he had no one to help him into the pool when the healing waters were stirred. In a sense he was communicating a sense of futility, that he would forever be held captive by his condition and situation. Although he came to the pool wanting to be healed, he wasn't sure how that healing could come to be.

That is how it is for many couples whose relationships have been torn asunder by cyberporn. Many couples are wounded by the breach of fidelity in the relationship and do not know how to find healing. It is not a lack of belief in the power of God to heal the relationship. It is not a lack of belief that forgiveness is possible. It is being immobilized by the breach of trust.

Most couples want to repair the relationship. They want to reestablish trust and commitment. They want to experience forgiveness and reconciliation. But feeling immobilized by the pain of their experience, they just do not know what to do.

To these couples we can imagine Jesus asking, "Do you want to get well?"

If so, he might say, "Get up! Pick up your mat and walk."

But how? If you want your marriage to survive, if you desire forgiveness and reconciliation, there is something you must do: trust in God enough to pick up the pieces of your broken relationship and get to the work of forgiveness.

Forgiveness and reconciliation don't just happen. They take action on your part. They are more than an attitude or a state of mind. There are tasks that must be done in order for forgiveness and reconciliation to occur.

And if doing something sounds strenuous, remember what it must have been like for that man who had been paralyzed for thirty-eight years. He encountered Christ. He experienced divine healing.

Consider this parable:

> "If a brother or sister sins, go and point out the fault, just between the two of you. If they listen to you, you have won them over. But if they will not listen, take one or two others along, so that 'every matter may be established by the testimony of two or three witnesses.' If they still refuse to listen, tell it to the church; and if they refuse to listen even to the church, treat them as you would a pagan or a tax collector."
>
> —Matthew 18:15-17

Christians are familiar with the admonition to go and confront the person who has sinned against them in order to seek reconciliation. But for most it is an uncommon strategy. Instead, most people who discover that their spouses are using cyberporn react in one of three ways: the ostrich response, the passive-aggressive response, and revenge and retribution.

The Ostrich Response
Like an ostrich with its head in the sand, we avoid a confrontation. We pretend nothing is wrong. We tell ourselves

to forget it, to let it go. There's no need to get upset. Maybe it's just a "guy thing."

The reality is that the harder you try to pretend nothing is wrong, the harder it is to be around your spouse. You don't feel happy or content. You feel a chasm of emotional distance. But you convince yourself this is better than a fight, and that if you ignore it, maybe it will just go away.

The Passive-Aggressive Response

You tell yourself there is no need to confront your spouse directly because he or she will come to realize intuitively that you know something. Your partner is wrong; you are right. If you lie in bed like a cold fish, maybe your partner will catch on that you know what's been going on and you disapprove.

Revenge and Retribution

Rather than confront your partner, you take every opportunity to take get back at him for hurting you. So if he offended you, you look for ways to offend him. If you are angry that he is looking at airbrushed, perfect women, you take it upon yourself to point out his imperfections—perhaps commenting on his balding head or the spare tire around his waist. Your comments are intended to cut him down and to make yourself feel better.

All three of these are common responses, but they fall far short of Jesus' expectations.

In Jesus' admonition from the gospel of Matthew, the burden of confrontation and confession is on the person who has been hurt, wronged, or violated. It may not seem fair, but that is what Christ calls us to do. But notice something else in that passage. Jesus is far less interested in who is right and who is wrong. His primary concern is getting people whose relationship has suffered a breach to find a way to work toward forgiveness and reconciliation.

You have the right to be hurt and angry if your partner has used the computer to engage in cybersex. No one should expect you to feel anything less. What you *do* with those feelings can either destroy you and your relationship or motivate you to muster the courage to approach your partner and begin the work of forgiveness and reconciliation.

But how?

Strategies for Forgiveness and Reconciliation

The path to forgiveness and reconciliation is a journey that begins one step at a time. When the bonds of marital trust are shattered and broken by an act of betrayal, this journey of healing is born out of a crisis—a crisis that attacks the marriage at its very core. The earth seems to shake and the heavens rumble, and suddenly the commitment and security the couple felt when they made their public marriage vows before God lie in pieces. Many wonder whether they can put the broken pieces of their marriage back together. They may feel confusion, hurt, sadness, and anger; feelings that suddenly appear but don't fade away overnight. The situation may seem desperate, even hopeless. Restoring hope can seem distant when a couple feels the painful wounds of betrayal.

Some couples survive the crisis, and their marriage becomes stronger than ever. For others, the wounds are so deep that the marriage is threatened. For some, the process of healing progresses rather smoothly and quickly. For many, however, it takes time to heal, as both partners must confront many obstacles and hurdles.

The emotional pain is real, and facing the pain is scary. Perhaps for the first time in the history of the marriage, many questions and issues are raised. There may be marital problems that have developed and evolved over the course of the marriage that have never been addressed. Or perhaps old childhood wounds once thought healed come to the surface.

Earlier attempts at resolution may have failed, causing a loss of faith and a fear of trying again. People lose faith in themselves, in their partners, and even in God. They may feel that their prayers over the years have gone unanswered, and the core of their faith is challenged.

As difficult as it may be, however, genuine forgiveness and reconciliation are possible.

Taking the Initial Steps

The first step in the process of forgiveness and reconciliation is to trust and believe that the relationship can be restored. Such an attitude communicates an expectation that change will occur.

Second, begin the journey with prayer. Let God intervene right from the start. God already knows of your pain. He wants to help. So pray alone, pray with each other, and ask others to pray for you.

Third, recognize common obstacles that hinder the process of forgiveness. Clients at The Hope and Healing Institute who struggled with forgiveness came to recognize factors that hindered their ability to achieve renewal in their relationships. These obstacles include the following:

- A lack of faith that prayer really works.

- A belief that God has given up and abandoned the relationship.

- Denying the problem. Avoiding the problem. Minimizing the impact of the problem on yourself and your family.

- Feeling unsafe to express real feelings, fearing it will cause your partner to relapse.

- Pride. Being too hesitant to turn to others for help.

- Making promises to stop engaging in online sexual activity and then repeatedly breaking the promise.

- Failure to take responsibility for your own actions, instead blaming other people or situations for the problem.

- Poor communication between partners.

- Not spending enough time working to save the relationship.

- Intense, unresolved anger.

It's important for couples to reflect on the obstacles that could hinder renewal and restoration of the relationship. Husbands and wives need to be honest and open with themselves and with each other. It can be very insightful to ask your spouse what he or she sees as a potential obstacle for you. This is risky. It can cause hurt feelings, and you may be shocked by what your spouse might say. But who knows you better than your spouse? Our tendency is to resist when someone mentions our faults. It's natural to be defensive. But if this form of sharing and communicating is done with a loving and respectful attitude, these walls of resistance begin to tumble down. Insights and revelations about each other begin to evolve, and this knowledge can go a long way toward healing the relationship.

> "To forgive is to set a prisoner free—and discover that the prisoner was you."
>
> —Lewis Smedes

Forgiveness as a Reciprocal Process

In her book *Forgiving the Unforgivable*, Beverly Flanigan has developed what she calls the "Transactional Model of Forgiveness."[6] This model is helpful in understanding how Christian couples can follow Christ's admonition in the eighteenth chapter of Matthew.

The key premise of Flanigan's transactional model is that every relationship has rules. These rules may be spoken or unspoken, but they are present and they affect the relationship in some way. She suggests that early on in relationships people begin to establish rules; for example, rules regarding honesty and truthfulness. If you break something that belongs to your spouse or a friend that is important to him, do you tell the truth or make up some excuse? If your spouse gets a new hairstyle that she really likes but you dislike, do you share your opinion or just agree with her? Every relationship has such rules, and they are not exactly the same for all relationships.

In addition to developing rules about issues such as honesty and truthfulness, every couple has developed some rule, whether spoken or unspoken, regarding the use of pornography and cybersex. If the rule establishes that this type of activity is not acceptable, then engaging in such activity is a violation of the rule in the marriage. Consequently the relationship is injured and trust is broken.

Flanigan's model emphasizes that the process of forgiveness and reconciliation is a reciprocal one in which both parties have an active role. To achieve genuine forgiveness and reconciliation, both parties must be involved. Both parties must recognize the violation. Both feel bad, but the injurer feels particularly guilty. However, both continue to believe that the rule between them was, and still is, good. One party made a mistake, that's all. However painful the mistake might be, both people in the relationship want to adhere again to the original rule they developed together. The contrite member can apologize and make promises. In response, the violated person can condemn or even punish the offender. In the end, apologies are accepted. The anger passes, and both people voluntarily agree to commit themselves to their original rule about how they should treat each other. Even if they decide to change the rule a little, both people agree to abide by that rule.

The model diagramed in the sidebar on page 90 illustrates the transactional or reciprocal nature of forgiveness and reconciliation. In marriage relationships, both partners have an active role. The process begins with a confrontation. The offended spouse must have the courage to confront the partner (see ch. 3). The pornography user must allow him- or herself to be held accountable. At this stage in the process both partners must spend considerable time discussing the nature of the offense and identifying what "rules" in the relationship have been broken as a consequence. Failure to adequately identify the rule will derail the forgiveness/reconciliation process. The offended spouse must be able to articulate the reasons why the behavior was wrong while the partner engages active listening skills. The partner must resist defensiveness and focus on understanding how the online sexual activity has affected the other person.

Portrayed as a diagram, this model may appear mechanical and void of emotion. On the contrary, though, it is imperative that the couple permits and encourages the healthy expression of emotion throughout the process of forgiveness and reconciliation. As described earlier in this chapter, people experience a wide range of emotions when they discover that their spouses are using Internet pornography. The offender must allow the partner to express these feelings. But the pornography user too is experiencing emotions, and those also must be expressed. Couples may need to seek professional guidance if both parties are experiencing deep resentment or rage. This transactional model is most effective when the pornography user comes to fully comprehend the nature of the offense and expresses true contrition, guilt, and sorrow for the behavior.

The goal of this transactional model is to reestablish trust. When a relational rule has been broken, the couple must work collaboratively either to recommit to the rule or to establish a new rule in its place. Reciprocally, wives and husbands must seek assurance and offer promises that the offense will not be repeated. Collaboratively, wives and husbands must covenant

A Transactional Model of Forgiveness and Reconciliation[7]

Offended Spouse	Pornography User
Accuses the pornography user of violating a relationship rule	Apologizes for breaking the rule
Summarizes the reasons the behavior was wrong	Listens and accepts
Expresses rage, sorrow, and a desire to punish	Accepts this punishment
Seeks assurance the offense will not be repeated	Promises to never repeat the offense
Accepts promises and demands no further "payment of debt"	Trusts that forgiveness is permanent
Recommitment to reestablished or new rules	Recommitment to reestablished or new rules

with each other that behavior in the future will be radically different, and trust that the forgiveness is permanent.

Action Steps in the Reciprocal Process

To forgive and to reconcile are "action words" requiring people to engage their emotional and spiritual energy to heal and save the relationship. Each partner plays a critical role in making this happen. Let's take a look at important actions for both partners that will facilitate this process.

For the Offended Spouse

1. Pray for your partner and yourself every day. Pray for renewed trust. Pray for honesty and openness.

2. Be patient. Change takes time, especially if the problem is deep-seated. Sometimes relapse is part of recovery. This is not an excuse to repeat the offense, but you have to be realistic. Try to be understanding, even though it may hurt to hear of a relapse. Communicate to your partner what form of relapse is totally unacceptable. Working toward reconciliation is about facing reality, not denying it.

3. Expect your partner to change and express that expectation clearly. Be loving but also firm.

4. Give yourself permission to have your feelings. You have a right to your feelings; they are yours. If you have been hurt, then you have a right to feel hurt. If you are angry, it's OK to be angry. Let your feelings out instead of bottling them up inside. Don't be ashamed or embarrassed to express your feelings. Cry them out if you need to. Let your partner know exactly how you feel. Clearly understanding the depth of the pain that has been caused can help prevent your partner from acting out again.

5. Give yourself permission to take your time to heal as well. Recovery is often focused on the pornography user's problem, and partners are left out of the healing process. This leads to isolation and puts them at risk for depression. Find trusted people you can talk to about how you are doing as well.

6. Try to understand and recognize that you might need to make some changes in the marriage as well. Listen to your spouse's concerns. Talk about concerns with an attitude of openness. Work together and support each other in every step of this journey.

For the Pornography User

1. Take responsibility for your actions and communicate clearly to your partner what it is you are apologizing for. Avoid *ifs, ands,* or *buts.* The process of forgiveness and reconciliation will be derailed if you use language that shifts blame or responsibility onto your partner. The word *if* is particularly damaging. For example, saying "I'm sorry if this upset you" does very little to encourage forgiveness. You are implying that you do not know whether you did anything wrong. The word *but* also confounds the problem because it declares that anything you said before was meaningless. For example, if you say, "You know I love you and prefer to be with you. I know I shouldn't have looked at those pictures, but I was horny and you didn't want to have sex." The "but" is a clear signal to your wife that perhaps you are trying to blame her and that you may not be as loving and loyal as you suggest.

2. Pray for your spouse's healing as well as your own. Pray that you may be able to help your partner to trust you again. Recognize that your spouse is going through recovery, just as you are, and be patient. Ask what he or she needs from you to be able to rebuild trust. Communicate directly and don't dance around the issues.

3. Ever heard the sayings "The proof is in the pudding" or "Actions speak louder than words"? That's especially true in recovery. Forgiveness is more likely to occur when your spouse sees you making real changes—perhaps a change in the way you act or communicate. The best way to build forgiveness is to put your partner's needs before your own. Demonstrate sincere repentance by explaining how you are going to change your attitudes and behaviors in the future. Give specific examples, like "I will make sure I have deleted all pornography on the computer, every picture," or "I've changed my computer screen name so the people

I have previously chatted with will no longer be able to contact me. I'm breaking off all relationships I developed while online." Keep in mind that relationships and feelings are very fragile. If you make a promise to change, you must do your best to honor this commitment. Broken promises create doubt and anger and undermine trust. After a while, defensive walls go back up and hope is lost.

4. Remember your marriage vows. They were made for a reason. Go back and look at the vows you made to each other. This can help reinforce the commitment you made. It can help remind you why you married your spouse in the first place and put the relationship back in focus. Remember that your life partner loves you more than any pornographic image you have ever looked at.

5. Talk about your feelings. Many people struggle to talk about their feelings. But their partners truly appreciate the effort. It's a way of expressing care and concern. Entrusting your spouse with your feelings is a way of showing that you care about him or her. Talk about the good days you are having and the battles you have won. Talk about any struggles to give in to the temptation of pornography. Be honest and sincere. Ask how your spouse is feeling about the progress you are making, and how he or she is coping. Listen carefully as your spouse expresses feelings. Communication needs to be a two-way street. Remember that mutual sharing will help rebuild trust.

6. Talk to your pastor and get professional counseling. Participate in a support group or Bible study. It is important to develop a network of people you can talk with and who can hold you accountable for change. Reach out to others who are supportive and who can relate to your struggles. Husbands and wives feel better when they see their spouses reaching out for help. Try to overcome the feeling you have to fix the problem yourself. You need more than your

partner for support. Your spouse needs to understand and work through his or her own feelings as well as trying to understand yours. A humble approach will go a long way toward rebuilding trust.

Depression and Anxiety Take Their Toll

Depression and anxiety are the most common emotional states reported by those who discover marital infidelity, including the discovery that their partners have breached the marriage covenant by viewing pornography online or engaging in an "online affair." Such a discovery often leads to mood and anxiety disorders.

The National Institute of Mental Health has identified key symptoms that indicate the presence of depression and/or anxiety.[8]

Warning Signs of Depression

- Persistent sad, anxious, or "empty mood" feelings of hopelessness, pessimism
- Feelings of guilt, worthlessness, helplessness
- Loss of interest or pleasure in hobbies and activities that were once enjoyed, including sex
- Decreased energy, fatigue, being "slowed down"
- Difficulty with concentrating, remembering, making decisions
- Insomnia, early-morning awakening, or oversleeping
- Appetite and/or weight loss or overeating and weight gain
- Thoughts of death or suicide; suicide attempts
- Restlessness, irritability
- Persistent physical symptoms that do not respond to treatment, such as headaches, digestive disorders, and chronic pain

An Update on Kathy and Tom

Kathy and Tom made very good progress in reconciling their relationship. Kathy worked very hard to forgive Tom while he worked to regain her trust. There were days of tension and even self-doubt, but they made a commitment to change, trusted God, and celebrated successes together. Tom was still tempted from time to time to return to pornography. Once in a while he slipped up and looked at pornography on the Internet. Each time he felt bad, told Kathy of his relapse, and they prayed for healing. Tom knew he would be tempted, but each time he resisted, he grew stronger, and the grip of pornography weakened.

Both identified obstacles to change right at the beginning. Tom was a proud man who was humbled when his secret came out. When confronted by Kathy, he apologized. Tom felt ashamed and embarrassed. He knew he had violated the marriage covenant. It took him time to understand and express these feelings to Kathy, and he shared one feeling at a time. Kathy worked hard to understand and overcome her anger. In time, her hurt and anger began to subside. Tom became a better listener and was able to grasp the depth of Kathy's emotional pain. She appreciated being able to express her feelings to Tom without him becoming angry with her. Together they worked at trusting God and began to spend more time nurturing their relationship. These steps helped them to move beyond the pain to experience genuine forgiveness and reconciliation.

Questions for Reflection and Discussion

1. If forgiveness doesn't mean forgetting, how will you know if you have truly forgiven?

2. Some people respond to online infidelity with an outburst of anger. Others experience an inner bitterness with little outward expression of hurt. How can this kind of response be more destructive than an outburst?

3. Should people disclose online sexual behavior to their spouse or partner even if doing so may cause that person more hurt?

4. How should you handle repeat offenses?

Chapter 5

What Were You Thinking?

A Question of Repentance

Bill's Story

I grew up with pornography. My friends in high school all looked at dirty magazines and my dad had subscriptions to both *Playboy* and *Penthouse*. In a way I just figured that it was "normal." I never considered pornography to be a big deal. At least, not until now.

As I write this, I am sitting alone in my new one-bedroom apartment, wondering what my wife and three children are doing back at home. How I wish I were with them! How I wish I could go back in time and undo all my stupid mistakes. How I wish I had thought more clearly of what I was doing that got me into this mess.

My fourteen-year-old daughter actually made the discovery. The laptop I had purchased for the kids to use for their homework had crashed, and, facing a deadline for a school project, she used the computer in my home office to search for some clip art. That's how she discovered my collection of pornography. And it wasn't just one or two pictures. I don't think I could even count the number of pictures I had downloaded over the years. These were not just pictures of scantily clad women. The stuff I looked at was hardcore.

My sweet little girl realized within seconds that her dad was sick. Sick and perverted. She hasn't spoken to me since.

I can still hear my wife's voice echo in my mind as she berated me: "What were you thinking?"

The reality is, I wasn't thinking. I wasn't thinking about what I was doing and how my behavior would affect my marriage or my family. And I definitely wasn't thinking about how it would affect my relationship with God.

I have used pornography since I was a teenager. My wife didn't approve, so I couldn't subscribe to magazines like my father did. Instead, I used the Internet. I would spend at least two hours a day surfing through porn sites and finding chatrooms to meet people to "trade" pictures with. Typically, I would wait until the kids had gone to bed and my wife was watching TV. I would tell her I needed to go upstairs and use the computer for work. Some of the time I actually had work to do, but that was a rare occasion. It got to a point where I considered this to be my "private time." With the kids asleep, the wife tired and preoccupied with the television, it was the perfect opportunity to be alone. At first I felt really guilty about lying to my wife. But over time the guilt was displaced by the thought that I deserved some private time.

When we first got the Internet, I never looked at porn sites when the family was around. But as time went on, I began to take a few more chances. Initially I always made sure the door was closed, but after a while I wouldn't bother. I would just listen carefully for anyone coming up the stairs. I got very good at hiding the pornography if I thought there was a chance I could get caught. It was sort of like a game, and I grew ever more confident in my ability to keep it all a secret. Of course there was the chance of getting caught, but the risk made the game more exciting. It was being naughty, taking chances, and getting away with something.

Like many men, I tricked myself into believing what I was doing wasn't that bad. I used to tell myself that I wasn't really hurting anyone. I figured I didn't really know these girls personally. If they were in these pictures without their clothes on, then that was their choice. They must really want to be seen this way or they wouldn't do it. After all, they were adults. No harm. Besides, my wife wouldn't dress the way they did. I tried to get her to dress the way I thought was sexy, and she wouldn't do it. I figured if my wife wouldn't dress or act like them, there was no harm in just looking at a few pictures now and then; pictures of women who seemed so willing and confident.

I didn't really feel like I was cheating either. I told myself over and over again that it was just for fun. The more I told myself this, the more I believed it. Eventually I convinced myself that what I was doing was acceptable.

There were some times when I thought I was losing control and would make a decision to stay away from the computer. But that would last no more than a week or so. I found myself thinking about pornography a lot when I was home, at work, and sometimes even at church. My mind would wander during the pastor's sermon and I'd think about when the next opportunity would present itself. I know it sounds crazy, but it's true. What was I thinking?

I wasn't thinking about my wife. I wasn't thinking about my children. I wasn't thinking about God. I wasn't thinking I had a problem. But I did. And as a result I lost my family.

Stinking Thinking Makes for Rotten Relationships

In many ways, human behavior is the result of what people think or believe about themselves and others. Our thoughts, beliefs, assumptions, and expectations direct how we behave. When our thoughts are rational (that is to say, accurate), we behave in rational ways. For example, when a husband attempts to initiate sexual intimacy and is told by his wife that she has a headache, his brain immediately begins to sort through lots of information: she has a history of migraines; migraines seem to run in her family; when she gets a migraine she feels sick to her stomach; what she needs is peace and quiet; the migraines never seem to last more than a day or two. With this information, the husband rationally takes action. He offers to call the doctor; he makes sure she is comfortable; he makes sure the kids are playing quietly.

But if there is a faulty or irrational thought process, the interaction between husband and wife could become severely distorted. If he believes that she is just avoiding him; if he interprets her response to be an indication that she is "frigid" and uninterested in sex; if he believes that she does not enjoy moments of physical and sexual intimacy, the entire scenario could become explosive.

God has created humans with the capacity to think. We have the ability to reason, solve problems, and examine issues from various points of view or perspectives. By divine design, we have the wonderful ability to correct our assumptions, beliefs, or expectations. And in correcting our thought patterns, we have the capacity to alter our behavior. When faced with a problem situation, humans are capable of thinking about the nature of the problem and considering a multiplicity of ways to resolve it. All by God's design.

In the 1950s, psychologists, including Albert Ellis and Aaron Beck, discovered the importance of irrational or faulty thinking and its effect on human behavior.[1] Based on vast empirical research, psychologists use a method of intervention known as "cognitive behavioral therapy" to assist people with their problems. Initially used as a treatment model for depression, cognitive behavioral therapy (CBT) has been used to help people cope with (and change) a wide variety of problems in life, including problems associated with online sexual activity and sexual addictions.

Cognitive behavioral therapy is based on the important principle that thoughts, belief systems, and assumptions affect human emotions and behavior. The primary goal of CBT is to help people identify irrational, inaccurate, faulty, or destructive thought patterns and replace them with thoughts that are more positive, realistic, and healthy. This is more complicated than just developing a "positive thinking" approach or "looking on the bright side." It entails learning to identify "stinking thinking" and to discover alternative, more realistic, rational interpretations.

Sometimes people are consciously aware of their thoughts and perspectives. Other times they may be unaware how their thought processes impact their emotional life and decision-making. Many people who struggle with pornography are oblivious to how their faulty thought process fuels their cybersexual behavior. Three of the most common, and by far the most dangerous, erroneous thoughts include minimization, justification, and "musterbating."

Minimization

Perhaps the most foul and stinky of all irrational thoughts in regard to pornography is this: "It's not that big a deal."

It *is* a big deal.

In the first place, pornography victimizes people. The vast majority of pornography depicts people engaged in what appear to be consensual sexual experiences. The persons depicted seem to be enjoying the experience and appear comfortable with being filmed and photographed. The sad reality is that many of them are forced to participate, manipulated through drugs, or threatened with bodily harm if they do not participate.

Second, pornography affects marital relationships. Research indicates that most men do not believe that their use of pornography has had a negative effect on their relationships.[2] However, when researchers explored their wives' experience, 100 percent of them felt that their husbands' use of pornography has had a harmful effect on the marriage.[3]

Third, pornography affects the individual. Research indicates that it is possible to develop an addiction to pornography. What may have started as recreational use becomes an obsession. Like a drug, the individual uses pornography more frequently than intended. The type of material viewed escalates from erotica to hard core. In order to achieve the same level of sexual arousal as before, the individual requires pornographic images that are increasingly more intense and graphic. The individual begins to disregard responsibilities at home or work as time and energy are absorbed in the use of pornography. The individual continues using pornography even while recognizing that it is having a harmful effect on the individual and on his or her marriage.

Justification
Christians know that the use of pornography is a sexual sin that dishonors God. They know that using pornography distorts their relationship with God and potentially with their spouse and family. But they continue to use it. The choice

to use pornography is driven by a negative thought process known as justification. Justifications are excuses that echo inside a person's mind, giving an excuse to use pornography. In most cases, however, the thought process is faulty. Bill knew that using porn was wrong, but he exercised very little self-control or restraint. He justified what he was doing by allowing irrational and incorrect thoughts to direct his use of porn.

These are some of the most common justifications:

- "It's not like I don't love my wife. It's just for fun."
- "I just need sex more than my wife does."
- "It's not as bad as guys who go to prostitutes."
- "It could be worse. I could be having a real affair."
- "If I was getting more sex at home, I wouldn't need to do this."
- "At least it's not kiddy porn."
- "It helps me relax."
- "I'm lonely and I get to talk with others who know what I'm going through."
- "I only look at pictures once a week; it's not like I have a real problem."
- "If I don't masturbate regularly, I feel like I'm going to explode."

Musterbating

No, it's not a typo. This is not about masturbation. This kind of stinking thinking is about people's faulty expectations wherein they put unreasonable demands on themselves and others. Albert Ellis calls this type of faulty thinking "musterbating."[1] People rationalize their use of pornography if they believe their expectations are not being met. The thought processes of those who "musterbate" reflect a sense of what "must" or "should" be occurring in their sexual relationship. In a sense, they believe there are certain rules in regard to sex. When the rules are not being followed, there is disappointment and frustration.

Couples need to discover what these rules are and determine whether there is common agreement or if the expectations are unreasonable. For example, a husband might believe that in a healthy marriage, a man and a woman should make love three times per week. The wife, however, might believe that sexual contact in a healthy marriage should occur once per week. The issue is not over who is right and who is wrong. Both partners have expectations and rules in regard to the frequency of sexual intimacy. However, if one or both of them maintains the position that his or her view is correct and the other's is faulty, there is potential for conflict. If the couple is not able to communicate and come to an agreement, there will be unresolved conflict.

The use of pornography introduces and reinforces faulty expectations. By viewing pornographic material or partici-pating in chatrooms or newsgroups, a person develops beliefs and attitudes regarding sex and sexuality. Although this information is usually inaccurate, the individual develops a sense that what they are experiencing is normative. The individual develops beliefs about the "rules" of sex; over time these beliefs become solidified and inflexible.

For example, in pornography women are typically portrayed as multi-orgasmic and as insatiable in their sexual desire. A man who repeatedly looks at such depictions may develop a sense that his wife "should" have multiple orgasms and "should" be interested in sex far more frequently. Similarly, a man who views pornography that portrays women crying out in orgasmic ecstasy may develop a rule that this is the epitome of expressing sexual satisfaction. With such an expectation, the husband will be disappointed if his wife's experience is more subdued.

Evaluating Bill's "Stinking Thinking"

The story at the beginning of this chapter demonstrates how faulty assumptions about pornography and "stinking thinking" led to an escalation of sexually inappropriate behavior.

Bill's use of pornography was getting out of control. Over time, he began to desire more and more pornography. Looking at a few pictures no longer satisfied his craving. In his mind, he needed more. It became difficult to control this desire and stop himself. He justified his actions, which led to lying to his wife about why he was going to the bedroom at night. Sometimes he really planned on working on the computer. But more often than not, he used the work excuse to cover his tracks. He even started to tell his wife he needed to work on the computer several hours before he actually went to his bedroom. As he practiced deception he became more confident. Lying to his wife became "comfortable." As Bill stated, "I grew ever more confident in my ability to keep it all a secret."

Bill's deception was very conscious. He began to lie and to justify his lying. He tried to block out any guilt and shame. At first, this was hard to do. He felt very guilty. But like many others, Bill's use of pornography became obsessive. He found it very difficult to control himself and stop.

As Bill became more comfortable surfing the Internet for pornography, he also took more chances. He began to look at pornography when his children were home, a boundary he had previously been unwilling to violate. He convinced himself he would not get caught. Although he felt guilty knowing the children were upstairs in their rooms next to his room, he began to feel less guilty over time. He began to believe that since he had never been caught, he had perfected his strategy. He convinced himself that the children would never walk in on him. Just in case they did, he planned a strategic response. When he anticipated a problem, rather than eliminate the behavior itself, he found ways to perpetuate his situation. He learned how to quickly cover up the pictures on the computer monitor so that no one would know what he had been looking at. This only magnified the risk that his behavior would escalate.

Feeling less guilty over time is a common dynamic in the escalation of an individual's use of pornography. It's another example how justification or rationalization can deaden feelings of guilt in the quest of fulfilling sexual desire. Bill felt some guilt when looking at pornography, but he compartmentalized it—simply made the guilt go away for a while so he could continue. He told himself these were just pictures. He convinced himself that it was normal for women to act and dress like the women in the pictures, and when his wife did not meet this expectation, he became angry with her and felt rejected. He turned to the pictures for comfort and pleasure, making one excuse after another.

This is a common sequence of events. Guilt usually follows the use of pornography, and sometimes even deters an individual from looking at it for a period of time. But once the desire returns and grows in strength and power, justification returns, and the cycle is repeated—sometimes over and over again within a very short period of time. Others may have a pattern that is less frequent: perhaps looking at pornography for a couple of hours during the week instead of once a day. Regardless of the frequency of use or the amount of risk taking, the pattern of escalation continues.

Bill's excitement for pornography waxed and waned. He began to escalate by going to pornography sites on a regular basis, identifying his favorite sites so he could go back over and over again, collecting pictures and then masturbating to them. When his use of pornography was reinforced by the pleasure he achieved through masturbation and orgasm, his desire became even stronger. Eventually this wasn't enough for Bill as he discovered chatrooms and started sharing fantasies he had about his wife and other people with others. Ultimately, he justified chatroom conversation as acceptable because he didn't know anyone personally. And besides, other men were doing it too.

Bill knew his behavior was wrong. At times his desire to stop was very strong, and sometimes he would win this battle. There were times he clicked on the computer, was tempted to go to a pornography site, but did not go. When this happened, he felt relieved and good about his decision. He prayed for self-control. When attending church, he felt ashamed and guilt-ridden, often feeling as if the pastor's sermons on sin were directed to him.

But sometimes problems get out of control. The intensity of the escalation process catches people off guard. What first may appear to be one small, harmless justification leads to a web of lies and secrecy. This process caught Bill off guard. He felt as if he'd been ambushed from behind. The destructive lure and power of pornography hit him when his guard was down and held him captive.

Bill fought hard to face these issues, and today he is stronger than when he first discovered Internet pornography. He freely admits it is a tough battle. He has relapsed and used pornography again. Each time he has had the courage to commit to change. He has been able to identify his thought patterns and assumptions about pornography and how they reinforced and escalated his behavior. This awareness and courage will help him in the fight to win this battle.

Scriptural Guidance for Repentance

One day Peter and John were going up to the temple at the time of prayer—at three in the afternoon. Now a man who was lame from birth was being carried to the temple gate called Beautiful, where he was put every day to beg from those going into the temple courts. When he saw Peter and John about to enter, he asked them for money. Peter looked straight at him, as did John. Then Peter said, "Look at us!" So the man gave them his attention, expecting to get something from them.

Then Peter said, "Silver or gold I do not have, but what I do have I give you. In the name of Jesus Christ of Nazareth, walk." Taking him by the right hand, he helped him up, and instantly the man's feet and ankles became strong. He jumped to his feet and began to walk. Then he went with them into the temple courts, walking and jumping, and praising God. When all the people saw him walking and praising God, they recognized him as the same man who used to sit begging at the temple gate called Beautiful, and they were filled with wonder and amazement at what had happened to him.

While the man held on to Peter and John, all the people were astonished and came running to them in the place called Solomon's Colonnade. When Peter saw this, he said to them: "People of Israel, why does this surprise you? Why do you stare at us as if by our own power or godliness we had made this man walk? The God of Abraham, Isaac and Jacob, the God of our fathers, has glorified his servant Jesus. You handed him over to be killed, and you disowned him before Pilate, though he had decided to let him go. You disowned the Holy and Righteous One and asked that a murderer be released to you. You killed the author of life, but God raised him from the dead. We are witnesses of this. By faith in the name of Jesus, this man whom you see and know was made strong. It is Jesus' name and the faith that comes through him that has completely healed him, as you can all see.

"Now, brothers and sisters, I know that you acted in ignorance, as did your leaders. But this is how God fulfilled what he had foretold through all the prophets, saying that his Messiah would suffer. Repent, then, and turn to God, so that your sins may be wiped out, that times of refreshing may come from the Lord."

—Acts 3:1-19

The book of Acts is perhaps one of the more neglected books of the New Testament. Most are familiar with the gospels— Matthew, Mark, Luke, and John—that describe the events of Jesus' birth, ministry, death, and resurrection. Many stop reading there, assuming that the story ends with Jesus' resurrection. But there's more to the story.

While the gospels end with the stories of Jesus' resurrection, the book of Acts begins and ends with stories about the ongoing miracle of the resurrection of others. Although we do not have people raised from literal graves as was Jesus, nevertheless we have people raised from certain kinds of graves.

Just as the gospels conclude with the message that crucifixion and death do not have the final word, the book of Acts proclaims that the power of resurrection, by the grace of the Holy Spirit, is still at work. The final words about life are not lameness, deafness, blindness, disease, or physical and mental disabilities; rather, the final words about life are health, strength, sight, and vitality. Jesus offers the power of his victorious resurrection through his life-giving Spirit. It is God's intention to continue the process of resurrection so that in place of discouragement and defeat, people can turn their lives around. By the grace of Jesus Christ, we can experience new life.

But how? How might we experience the power of resurrection and renewal?

Insight comes from Peter's sermon at Solomon's Colonnade in the temple, where he urges the crowd, "Repent then, and turn to God, so that your sins may be wiped out, that times of refreshing may come from the Lord."

What does it mean to repent? It means to change. The key to resurrection and new life is change. When the author of the book of Acts described this event in Jerusalem he used one of the classic Greek words for repentance: *metanoia*. It means a "change of mind" or transformation of thought patterns. One of the first steps toward renewal and resurrection is a change in our ways of thinking.

The lame man in this passage in Acts had to change his way of thinking in order to experience renewal. We're told he had been lame from birth and that he was now about forty. Since wheelchairs had not yet been invented, he had to be carried wherever he wanted to go. Indeed, some friends apparently were in the habit of carrying him to the gate each morning so that he could beg for money.

This man's entire identity was shaped by his physical condition. He viewed himself as nothing more than a beggar. His physical condition made it difficult for him to see himself as equal to others. But Peter and John saw beyond that when the man asked them for some spare change at the temple gate. While others might have averted their eyes or deliberately avoided the encounter, Peter "fixed his gaze upon him," as did John. Beyond this man's physical limitations they saw a human being, a child of God. And they were about to help him gain the same perspective.

"Silver or gold I do not have, but what I do have I give you. In the name of Jesus Christ of Nazareth, walk." Peter took him by the hand and raised him up. Soon the man was walking and leaping and praising God, entering the temple with them to worship, to the amazement of all.

Here we see the power of the resurrected Jesus still at work—not only in healing this man's physical condition, but also in changing his way of thinking about himself and the world. This man was overjoyed to change his entire self-image in order to live life as a whole man, healthy and well. He celebrated his renewal by leaping and jumping his way into the temple courts to worship God!

In many ways, those caught in the mire of pornography and cybersex are psychologically and spiritually handicapped. They have grown accustomed to think in certain ways. Caught in the deception and inaccuracy of their thoughts, they have become lame and powerless over their desires. They consider themselves to be paralyzed, unable to control their behavior.

This inaccurate self-perception is the result of inaccurate thoughts that have been allowed to echo within their minds, thoughts such as "It's not really hurting anyone," or "It's better to look at pictures than have a real affair," or "Using pornography is not as bad as using prostitutes," or "It's just for fun," or "At least I'm not using kiddy porn."

As described above, many of these thoughts reflect minimization, justification, and faulty expectations. Psychologically, they shape attitudes and behavior that are problematic and perhaps pathological. Repentance, therefore, begins with a change in an individual's thought process. It involves a thorough and honest evaluation of one's thoughts, beliefs, and expectations.

Repentance, however, means more than just a change of mind. To be complete, repentance also requires a change in behavior. We know little about the lame beggar after the healing incident except that he entered the temple praising God. However, we can imagine that Peter and John would have advised him to live a productive life as a follower of Jesus Christ. Not only would this man need to change his way of thinking about himself, he would also need to change his behavior, his ways of acting and doing. No longer could he sit around the temple gate waiting for handouts. He had to change his daily routine, his way of living.

For Christians who have used pornography, a change in thoughts, beliefs, and expectations is essential. In addition, there is a critical need to change sexual behavior. Complete repentance involves not only harnessing thoughts but controlling behavior.

Christians need to approach their sexuality as a spiritual discipline. Unfortunately, our culture encourages the false belief that humans have little control over urges and desires. It conditions people to believe that sexual fantasy and unbridled desire are part and parcel of being human. The reality is that God gives us the power (and the freedom) to make choices. Christians, therefore, must choose to engage their sexuality in the way God intended. Sex is not "naughty" or ungodly. God created men and women as sexual creatures that respond to physical beauty, and we are to celebrate and enjoy our sexuality rather than debasing it and reducing it to nothing more than lust.

As a spiritual discipline, we have to develop power over our sexual desires. Some people excuse their behavior by "thinking" that it is beyond their control, that the images are too provocative, too alluring, too tempting. And to a degree this is true. The images are powerful. The temptation is real.

But the power is not beyond anyone. You can make choices and you are responsible for your own behavior. This important fact must echo within your mind and soul: God has given you willpower, and it is for you to exercise and utilize that will to resist sexual temptation.

The book of Acts has twenty-eight chapters, and the twenty-eighth chapter ends abruptly—as if the rest of the story is to be continued. That story has been continuing for twenty centuries. The story of the ongoing power of God continues in the faith community. It continues wherever people are open to God's Spirit and are willing to be raised from the dead by the power of Christ, willing to repent, to change in thought, behavior, and expectation. Such persons are proof of the ongoing power of resurrection.

What Do *You* Think about Pornography?

If you have Internet access, you need to evaluate your thoughts about Internet pornography. Do you believe the use of pornography is morally right or wrong? Does it honor God? Does it help you in your life of discipleship? Does it help your relationships?

If you judge the use of pornography to reflect moral and spiritual failure, you will be more hesitant to use pornography. On the other hand, if you think pornography is acceptable or "not that bad," you will probably be more tempted to look at it when given the opportunity.

In other words, how you think about pornography can dramatically affect your desire to use it or strengthen your willpower to resist it. That's true for any number of things. For example, most people are aware that the use of cocaine can stimulate pleasurable sensations throughout the body. But most people also believe cocaine use is wrong and should never be tried. They know this even without experimenting and taking a chance. The result? They have no temptation to use it. They never try it, not even once.

The pornography industry has tried to normalize the use of pornography. They want you to believe that pornography is harmless and even beneficial. In many ways the industry has been successful—many people believe that the use of pornography is a normal part of being human. We encourage members of the faith community, however, to reflect on and examine the impact pornography has had on their lives. By challenging yourself to think about your attitudes toward pornography, you will be better prepared to resist the temptation to use it.

The Three-Second Rule

It is vitally important to identify and catch faulty thoughts as soon as possible. The three-second rule is a simple tool you can use to control your thinking. Remind yourself that you have about three seconds to identify, catch, and change your thoughts. A single thought can lead to a series of thoughts and eventually to a sexual fantasy. The longer you dwell on pornographic images, the stronger your desire will be to act out what you are thinking. As your desire grows, you will try to justify and minimize your behavior. And, like pouring gasoline on a fire, making excuses will cause you to lose control of yourself. Keep in mind that it doesn't take very long to develop a very graphic and arousing sexual fantasy. And it's harder to control sexual thoughts once they become arousing and pleasurable. Let's use Bill's situation to illustrate how the three-second rule might work for you.

When Bill was home at night with his family, he began to anticipate going upstairs and using the computer as soon as his children went to bed. This was a mental trigger to think about using pornography. He'd say to himself, "The kids are going to bed. This is my opportunity to use the computer and check my favorite porn site." Using the three-second rule, as soon as he recognized this thought, he stopped and changed it to, "This is time for me and my wife to spend together."

Here's another example. Bill was at work, daydreaming and thinking about the end of his workday. He caught himself thinking, "Tonight I need some time to relax; I can't wait to get online." He countered this thought after recognizing by praying, "Dear Lord, deliver me from the desire to use pornography." Sometimes he would bring out his Bible and read a passage that was meaningful to him. This would immediately break the cycle of unhealthy thinking before he found himself drifting off into a sexual fantasy.

Overhearing the guys at work talking about pornography triggered this thought: "See, it's normal; these guys do it." Bill countered the thought with "It's wrong, I need to walk in the Spirit. I don't want to be like other guys."

At times Bill found himself thinking, "I'm so stressed out. I need a release." He countered this thought by telling himself, "I need to talk to my wife about my stressful day" or "I'm going to work out when I get home."

Whatever your situation might be, try to identify your most common thoughts or beliefs and write down a counter thought or belief, like Bill did. It takes practice. The harder you try and the more you practice, the better you'll be able to catch your thoughts and replace them with something healthier in under three seconds. If it takes longer than three seconds, that's OK—don't feel guilty or believe you are failing. You'll get the hang of it with time, and you'll start to see the results. Remember that the goal is to identify unhealthy thoughts and replace them with healthier, more productive ones as quickly as possible.

Thoughts and Counter Thoughts

Following is a list of the most common thoughts, beliefs, and justifications people use when looking at pornography and some examples of counter thoughts. Look at the list carefully and see if you can identify any of these in yourself or your loved ones. Approach the list with an open mind. Perhaps you'll come up with a better counter thought that is more suited to your situation than the example included below. This is how you can begin to challenge and attack your way of thinking. Try to replace the dysfunctional thought or belief with a positive counter thought. Over time, your pattern of thinking will change. And when your thoughts and beliefs are healthier, you will feel better about yourself.

Thought: I know it might be wrong, but I could be doing worse things. I could be drinking, staying out all night, or even having an affair.

Counter thought: There is no redeeming value in pornography. It does not honor God. It debases rather than celebrates the God-given gift of sexuality.

Thought: Where do they find all those attractive women in the pictures and movies? They must really like sex!

Counter thought: Many of the women in those pictures have histories of sexual abuse. Many are coerced to participate and others face severe physical abuse if they refuse.

Thought: Other guys look at this stuff. It must be pretty normal.

Counter thought: As a Christian, I am called to a high moral standard. I'm going to walk in the Spirit and strive to be a role model for others.

Thought: No one will find out. It's a secret.

Counter thought: It's not a secret. God knows.

Thought: If I were getting more sex at home, I wouldn't need this. I need some release.

Counter thought: Marriage is more than just sex. My spouse is my life partner. I need to talk to her about this aspect of our relationship.

Thought: It's true I masturbate while looking at pornography, but what guy hasn't?

Counter thought: I don't need to masturbate. I can control my urges and wait until I am with my wife to celebrate our marriage.

A Pastor's Perspective

Genesis 17 describes God's covenant relationship with Abraham. As a mark of the covenant, Abraham agreed to be circumcised, a procedure in which the foreskin of the penis is removed.

Although circumcision is no longer a requirement for membership in the Christian community, Christian men who have been circumcised can use circumcision as a reminder of their covenant relationship with God. Whether standing at a urinal, making love to your wife, or being tempted to masturbate, let your circumcision remind you that your behavior is to reflect that covenant relationship.

Stop, Drop, and Roll: Discovering and Correcting Dysfunctional Thoughts

Living in a sex-saturated society, it is important for members of the faith community to take time to assess and evaluate their thoughts regarding sex and sexual relationships. Especially those whose lives have been affected by pornography and cybersex must make an effort to identify potentially unhealthy, dysfunctional thoughts, beliefs, assumptions, and expectations.

Stop and Identify Thoughts, Beliefs, Assumptions, and Expectations

With your spouse or accountability partner, take time to brainstorm your thoughts about your sexual relationship and pornography. During this first step, make sure you don't get hung up on critical evaluation of the validity or veracity of your thoughts. This is brainstorming, not analysis. There are no "wrong" answers here. Later, of course, you may discover erroneous thoughts and choose to focus on an alternative interpretation. For now, focus your energy on articulating your thoughts.

The purpose of this step is to reveal the minimizations, justifications, and "musterbations" that contribute to the decision to use pornography. To begin this process, we encourage you and your partner to ask yourselves the following questions:

1. How frequently would you want to engage in sexual intimacy with your partner?

2. What are your expectations regarding initiation of sexual intimacy? Who should do what and when?

3. Consider five things about yourself that you might change in regard to sexual intimacy with your partner. Identify those statements that include the words "must" or "should."

4. Consider five things about your partner that you might change in regard to sexual intimacy. Identify those statements that include the words "must" or "should."

5. How has the use of pornography benefited or helped you?

6. How has the use of pornography benefited or helped your partner?

7. Has pornography helped you to better understand the needs/desires of the opposite sex? What have you learned?

8. If you have used Internet pornography, identify the excuses/explanations you have used to justify the behavior.

9. Have there been any fantasies that have emerged since you began using Internet pornography?

10. If you could choreograph a "perfect" sexual experience with your partner, what would be involved? Who would do what? Are any of your ideas associated with what you may have viewed in pornography?

Drop the Erroneous or Dysfunctional Thoughts

The intention of this step is to sort out healthy thoughts from those that may cause damage to the relationship. Couples need to approach this step by engaging the basic listening skills described in chapter 3. Enter into this step prayerfully and challenge yourself to avoid defensiveness.

For each of the responses to the questions above, you and your partner need to collaboratively decide the degree to which the thought, belief, or expectation is healthy or reasonable. Identify thoughts, attitudes, or expectations that may have been shaped by an experience with pornography. Recognize those that may reflect minimization, justification, or "musterbation."

Note that it is very difficult for most people to effectively evaluate whether their thoughts, beliefs, or expectations are dysfunctional. For that reason, it is very important to continue this exercise with your spouse or a professional counselor.

Roll These Thoughts into Healthier Alternative Thoughts

The challenge in this step is to transform dysfunctional thoughts into healthier, alternative thoughts that honor both the relationship and God.

This involves identifying an alternative interpretation to distorted ways of thinking. For example, if a husband's use of pornography has led him to the belief that "most women want sex more than my wife does," he may be erroneously thinking, "My wife never wants to have sex." A healthier alternative might be "My wife seems to be more interested in sex when . . ."

Questions for Reflection and Discussion

1. What do you think it means to repent?

2. Proverbs 16:18 says: "Pride goes before destruction, a haughty spirit before a fall." What does that tell us about the obstacles to repentance in regard to sexual sin?

3. Can a person simply "feel" repentant or must a person "show" repentance?

Chapter 6

Lost in the Wilderness

The Dangerous Terrain of Internet Chatrooms

Mary's Story

I am the mother of three wonderful children and a wife to a husband who works very hard to provide for our family. This is my second marriage. My first marriage lasted about five years. We married young and were both immature. We found our lives going in different directions: he wanted the fast life filled with material things and fun, and I wanted to settle down and have children. We quickly grew apart and divorced. My family found it difficult to accept the divorce, but that is partially my fault. I had given them the clear impression that things were fine. I was too embarrassed to admit that my marriage was falling apart.

A few years later I met Donald. He seemod like Mr. Right—an answer to prayer. My family loved and adored him and saw that I was beginning to feel happy again. We started our family and moved from an apartment to a house. Life seemed to be going along quite well. We both agreed that I would be a stay-at-home mother. The financial sacrifices were worth it. I felt I could give my children everything they needed, and I loved being a mother.

My story really begins when my youngest daughter started kindergarten. Our home seemed so quiet and empty. Yes, it provided me with some private time, but my kids seemed to be growing up way too fast, and I could sense that they didn't need me as much as when they were younger. There was loneliness, some guilt over feeling bad when I had the "perfect" life, and a sense that I was growing older.

I started working out because I had been putting on some weight, but exercise has never been something I looked forward to, so it didn't last very long. I wasn't too pleased with what I saw in the mirror, so I got a makeover, changing the color and length of my hair. I spent way too much money on new clothes. But none of it made me feel any better.

I was unhappy with myself, feeling older, feeling like my kids didn't need me as much, and wondering where my life was headed.

And my marriage? This is hard to explain, but things seemed to have changed over time. He was busy with work, putting in lots of hours. We seemed to be growing apart, gradually and slowly over time. The excitement we once had faded away. We drifted apart. I felt he was losing interest in me. I felt lonely, old, and unattractive.

Out of boredom I started using the Internet. I wasn't looking for pornography or anything distasteful like that. I'm not sure what I was looking for, but I can tell you that what I found almost ruined my life.

When I first went exploring online, I had no clue as to what danger awaited me. I was rather innocent and naive about the computer, especially the Internet. But once I figured out how to click a few buttons, I started writing letters to family and friends, and once in a while, I actually talked to my girlfriend online using something called instant messaging. You just make up a screen name, give it to your friend, put your friend's name on something called a buddy list, and then start chatting when you see them online. It was so easy and so fun. It really helped pass the time and gave me something to do. I felt I had graduated to the modern era of technology.

This is where my journey takes a sad turn. Actually, this is very embarrassing to talk about, but I'm determined to tell my story and deal with my guilt and shame. By telling my story, I hope other women can avoid the same mistakes I've made.

I remember one fall day where the leaves had turned colors and it seemed dark and gloomy. The kind of day when you just want to stay home, drink some coffee, and curl up with a good book. I was bored, somewhat lonely, and tired of all the housework. So I went online.

I wrote a few e-mails to friends, and then, just out of curiosity, I checked out the chatrooms listed by our Internet provider. It was amazing how many chatrooms there were with different titles and themes. Some rooms are created by the Internet provider, but many are made up by other people who use the same Internet company.

I started exploring. The first chatroom I went into was called "gardening." People were just talking about gardening, and everyone seemed friendly. I didn't say a word, and just watched the conversation unfold. When I say "talking," it just means people were typing their thoughts, and you can see what you and others type on the computer screen. When you enter a chatroom, sometimes people say "hello" or "welcome" to the room. It is entirely up to you if you want to respond back in some way.

Although "chatting" with people I couldn't see or know seemed awkward at first, I gradually became more comfortable and it didn't seem odd anymore. I could talk anonymously with people in the privacy of my own home. No one could actually see me or hear my voice, and it was sort of fun. Some people actually formed online friendships and would chat with each other whenever they were both online. The "regulars" in the garden chatroom seemed to know I was a "newbie"—a new person to the chatroom.

Over a period of weeks, I started exploring different kinds of chatrooms. Many of the chatroom names were overtly sexual and offensively explicit, and I was careful to stay away from them. I didn't even want to imagine what was going on in those rooms; it didn't appeal to me one bit. Instead, I went to a chatroom called "married and flirting." I was curious as to what went on there.

As soon as I entered the room, people I didn't even know tried to strike up a conversation with me or send one of those private instant messages. They were all men vying for my attention. Some introduced themselves by saying something quite sexual, while others were more polite. Men right away wanted to know my age, what I looked like, where I lived, and if I was happily married. It felt like guys were swarming all over me, and frankly, I liked the attention.

It became a matter of routine, after a while, that I would visit the "married and flirting" chatroom. Part of the experience, I admit, was rather distasteful. I'll never forget this one guy who would send me an instant message every time I signed on the computer. It was so annoying. He was relentless in asking for my personal picture and suggesting we meet offline for some conversation and fun. It always amazed me how fast some people wanted to chat over the phone and even meet in person when they didn't really even know me. I mean, how do you know these guys aren't stalkers, or worse? After all, they talked so graphically about sexual stuff. It was gross!

Some guys even sent pictures of themselves over the computer. Once in a while I would open the e-mail to see what they looked like. Some sent naked pictures of themselves, and I thought that was kind of gross. How could someone send a naked picture of themselves to someone they didn't even know? But the guys I chatted with assured me that many women send pictures like that, chat on the phone, and even meet in person. Maybe so, but that seemed dangerous to me, and sleazy. I wasn't that type of girl. Or was I?

One day I chatted online with a man who actually seemed very nice. I wasn't sure at first if he was genuine or if it was just a game to try to win my trust. He was married, had several children, and openly admitted he was bored in his marriage. Apparently, the intimacy in his marriage had been lacking for some time. We seemed to hit it off quite well. He never pressured me for pictures or phone calls, so my comfort level with him grew over time. It's funny how sometimes you can tell personal things about your life to people you've never met. Maybe it has to do with being anonymous. In any case, we developed an online friendship.

Part of me felt guilty talking to a man I didn't really know, but the more we chatted the more I felt I knew him. The more we chatted, the more I started believing that he knew me better than my own husband. The more we chatted, the more I started to think I was falling in love.

Looking back, I realize that we were both needy for some attention and affection. He seemed like a good listener so I shared some of my frustrations about my marriage. We were developing what I've come to learn is an online emotional affair. Who, me? An online emotional affair? It's embarrassing to admit, but yes, online emotional affairs do occur, and I'm living proof of how easily it can happen.

One day, he suggested that we had reached the point in our relationship where we should meet. I was very conflicted about this suggestion—and scared too. But a part of me wanted to see and hear from the person I had been sharing personal stories with. Initially I said no. But over the next few months my husband and I were having more and more disagreements, and I felt myself growing more distant from him. Having met someone online with whom I could talk so freely, why couldn't I have something similar with my husband? I began to tell myself that perhaps God wanted me to have a closer, more meaningful relationship with someone else.

Six months after our initial encounter in the chatroom, my new friend and I made plans to meet.

Not wanting to be seen, we arranged to meet at a restaurant about an hour away from my home. As I drove, I felt a hint of guilt knowing that I was taking a step away from my marriage. But the guilt was superseded by a desire to be emotionally close with someone. I was lonely and wanted desperately to be loved and cherished. I felt I deserved better in life.

As I approached the restaurant, I could feel the anticipation well up within me. I stopped at a traffic light and strained my eyes, wondering if I could catch a glimpse of the one who would rescue me from my dull existence. But my eye caught something else across the street from the restaurant: a church steeple with a cross.

I didn't notice the light turn green, nor did I hear the guy behind me honk his horn. The driver in that car actually got out of his vehicle and tapped on my car window. I was in tears. Sobbing. He asked if I was all right, and I assured him I was OK. But it was a lie. Something was terribly wrong. And if I had not seen that cross, it could have been a whole lot worse.

I turned the car around and headed home, crying most of the way. I needed to talk to someone, but who could understand what was going through my head and heart?

I drove straight to our church, hoping to talk to the pastor, but he was out of the office visiting some people at the hospital. And so I waited.

I waited in the sanctuary, trying to pull myself together. And I prayed.

Lost in the Wilderness: Chatrooms for the Lonely

The Internet, and specifically its array of chatrooms, is like a wilderness. It may be interesting to explore, but there is darkness lurking everywhere for those who are unaware of the dangerous traps that lie ahead. For many, the Internet seems like a harmless place. But many, like Mary, are led astray by their curiosity.

Mary was married, but she was also lonely. There was a void in her life that she did not understand, and sometimes she felt depressed. Her experience was difficult for her to talk about. Like many people, she found it challenging to talk about her marriage or admit she felt lonely or needy. She felt guilty, believing she should be content with life's circumstances, not wanting to come across as a complainer or ungrateful. Over time the joy and the glow of the wedding day had faded, but

Mary kept her feelings to herself. Mary's loneliness made her vulnerable in the wilderness.

There are many people online waiting for people like Mary to appear. They search the Internet, cruising chatrooms and trying to start up conversations. Some are very bold and demand sexual chat. This is a turnoff for many women. Others, cleverer in their approach, say the right things to make lonely people feel important. Hearing compliments from someone they don't even know can feel good to a lonely or needy person. It may seem odd or silly, but some people are attracted to this type of interaction. In a misleading way, the anonymity of the virtual interaction causes a person to feel safe. Identities are cloaked on the Internet, and the environment of chatrooms provides a place for people to interact with no measure of commitment.

Some men are very manipulative and deceptive, telling the women whatever she wants to hear. Mary's new friend was a good listener and came across as caring. This made Mary feel good. But the more you travel to the wilderness, the greater the risk of losing perspective on how the Internet is affecting your life. We all have needs, emotional and physical, and if these needs are not being met in a marriage relationship, the temptation to stray becomes stronger, especially over the Internet.

Some men are lonely too—just like Mary. These lonely people can visit chatrooms with names such as "Bored and Married," "Married and Flirting," "Hot Christian Wives," "Talk with a Pastor," "Listening Friend," and "Affairs and Cheating." In these chatrooms, such people can find each other and become emotionally attracted to one another. Loneliness is a very powerful emotion. It makes a person feel down—sad and depressed, unworthy and unloved. It's a hard thing to feel for any length of time.

Mary was vulnerable. Her judgment changed over time and she began to fill her need for companionship on the Internet. Even though she knew what she was doing was wrong, over time she let her guard down, taking more risks and justifying or rationalizing her behavior along the way.

The Internet is a very seductive place. Feelings can get hurt, and voids may be superficially filled. When Mary found her way out of the wilderness, she had to deal with a lot of guilt and shame. She had placed herself and her marriage at risk. Fortunately, she found the light, and the light guided her out of darkness.

A Pastor's Perspective

Mary came to see me one day. She asked if there was a woman she could talk to about something private. She'd feel more comfortable talking to a woman.

I knew exactly the right person to suggest.

Mary was embarrassed to talk about her experiences on the Internet. She felt intense and pervasive shame. But by recognizing her problem and seeking help, she was able to find her way out of the wilderness. She eventually came to understand what emotional needs she was trying to meet through the Internet, and she turned her heart and energies toward repairing her relationship with her husband.

Scriptural Guidance for Those Who Are Lost in the Wilderness

The desert and the parched land will be glad;
the wilderness will rejoice and blossom.
Like the crocus, it will burst into bloom;
it will rejoice greatly and shout for joy.
The glory of Lebanon will be given to it,
the splendor of Carmel and Sharon;

they will see the glory of the Lord,
the splendor of our God.

And a highway will be there;
it will be called the Way of Holiness;
it will be for those who walk on that Way.
The unclean will not journey on it;
wicked fools will not go about on it.

No lion will be there,
nor any ravenous beast;
they will not be found there.
But only the redeemed will walk there,

and those the Lord has rescued will return.
They will enter Zion with singing;
everlasting joy will crown their heads.
Gladness and joy will overtake them,
and sorrow and sighing will flee away.

—Isaiah 35:1-2, 8-10

Comfort, comfort my people, says your God.

Speak tenderly to Jerusalem, and proclaim to her
that her hard service has been completed,
that her sin has been paid for,
that she has received from the Lord's hand
double for all her sins.

A voice of one calling:
"In the wilderness prepare the way for the Lord;
make straight in the desert a highway for our God.

Every valley shall be raised up,
every mountain and hill made low;
the rough ground shall become level,
the rugged places a plain.

And the glory of the Lord will be revealed,
and all people will see it together.
For the mouth of the Lord has spoken. "

—Isaiah 40:1-5

It's easy to get lost in a wilderness. Mile after mile, the size and sameness is disorienting and discomforting. You climb hill after hill, hoping each one will provide a new perspective that will reveal the way home. Yet each hilltop provides the same view as the one before. You begin to despair that you will ever find your way out. You feel alone and vulnerable and frightened.

The Hebrew people knew the wilderness experience. After Moses led them out of bondage in Egypt, they wandered in the wilderness for forty years. When Old Testament authors speak of wilderness, they're evoking the memory of a time of lonesome wandering in a barren land; a time when the Hebrew people felt alone and forsaken by God.

A wilderness can be a physical reality, such as the wilderness in which the Israelites wandered for forty years or the place where Satan tempted Jesus after his baptism. But the Bible also uses "wilderness" as a metaphor for times when we feel lost and lonely. Times when we're in trouble and feel distant from God. Times when we venture into dangerous terrain and discover just how lost we are. At times like that, we cry out to God to rescue us.

These passages from the book of Isaiah speak of such a time. It was during the Babylonian exile, and the Hebrew people were feeling lost. In 587 B.C. the Babylonians had invaded the city of Jerusalem and destroyed the Temple of Solomon. Forced into exile, many of the Hebrew people were living in the barren land of Babylon. It was as if they were once again wandering in the wilderness.

In chapter 35, the prophet Isaiah describes what would happen if God would appear in the wilderness. The dry and barren land will burst forth in bloom, he says; waters will rush out to fill streams and pools; green grasses will grow. The wilderness will be transformed. In the midst of its vast desolation a road will be built; a highway so broad and so wide that it will show the people of God the way back home to Jerusalem. This highway will be visible from everywhere. It will be so easy to travel that no one will ever get lost in the wilderness.

That highway will save God's people from forever wandering hopelessly in the wilderness. When they travel on God's highway, they will know who they are and where they are to go. And they will know that this is God's highway, says Isaiah, because those who are blind will be able to see, those who are deaf will be able to hear, those who are lame will leap like deer, and those who cannot speak will sing for joy.

Jesus Christ is God's highway, God's presence in the wilderness.

Those whose lives have been affected by pornography and cybersex are lost in the wilderness. In the story at the beginning of this chapter you read about Mary, who went down the dangerous path of exploring cybersexual chatrooms. Many people find themselves lost in the wilderness terrain of cybersex and Internet pornography. By their own actions they have distanced themselves from marriage partners, from family, and from God. They feel lonely and hopeless. But there is hope. When they realize the mistakes they've made, when they realize just how lost they are, they begin to look for a way out of the wilderness, a path.

The way out of the wilderness is found in Jesus Christ.

Strategies for Finding Your Way Out of the Wilderness

Experts in the field of wilderness exploration will tell you that if you get lost, the key to survival is to stay calm. Those who panic tend to take action before thinking, jeopardizing their chances for survival. If you get lost, your chances for survival increase exponentially if you follow three primary survival strategies: First, get your bearings. Second, move in a constant direction (preferably using a compass). And third, keep scanning the horizon for signs of potential rescue.

Get Your Bearings

Once she had wandered into the dangerous terrain of Internet chatrooms, Mary soon discovered the trouble she was getting into. Finding her way out of the mess she had created required her to assess the situation. She knew she had made a mistake, that's for sure.

The primary means by which she was able to stay calm was prayer.

Mary's story is a marvelous example of an individual who, once she recognized her dilemma, turned immediately to God in prayer, asking God to strengthen her relationship with God and with her husband. This gave her focus. It allowed her to concentrate her focus on her Redeemer. And it allowed her to make an accurate assessment of what she had done.

Prayer and spiritual devotion helped Mary resist future temptations to reconnect with the Internet and search out relationships on the days she felt down and discouraged. Through prayer she came to realize that the Internet was not an option for coping with loneliness. Often people are tempted in their area of weakness or vulnerability. It's best for them to recognize that they will likely be tempted to relapse; this in itself provides individuals with strength to resist the temptation because they are less likely to be caught off guard.

The Prayer of the Prodigal

When experiencing significant shame, many Christians find it difficult to pray, not knowing what words to use. How does a person approach God in the aftermath of sexual sin?

Like the prodigal son, the first step is to go home to be greeted by a forgiving father. It will be a humbling experience, and you may find a scarcity of words and language to describe your emotions. We suggest, therefore, that in your prayers you do the following:

- **Center your thoughts on the majesty of God.** This is the great Creator, the maker of the heavens and the earth. This is the Creator who formed you in your mother's womb. Center your thoughts also on God's Son, Jesus Christ. By his birth, death, and resurrection, your sins are forgiven. By his sacrifice your relationship with God is restored. Then center your thoughts on the Holy Spirit, who has guided you to discover the error of your ways and who invites you to return to God. By centering your thoughts on God the Creator, Redeemer, and Sustainer, you will find the language to appropriately praise and celebrate your Lord. And in so doing, you will sense God embracing you, just as the prodigal son's father greeted his wayward child.

- **Make your confession.** This is not an exercise in informing God of your actions—God already knows what you have done. Rather it is an opportunity for you to conduct a full inventory of your sin. Focus on the effect your behavior has had on your relationship with God, with others, and its effect on you. Consider the manner in which you should have conducted yourself and recognize how far you were from that standard.

- **Celebrate forgiveness.** With tears of gratitude or a joyful smile, allow God's Spirit to wash you clean of your sin. Unlike times before, however, when you may have offered a glib and cursory confession, your current action is a pledge, a commitment to a different way of life. No longer will you offer prayers only in times of crisis or fleeting moments of remorse. Celebrate your renewed relationship with God through a spiritual discipline of daily prayer.

- **Ask for divine guidance.** Again, this is a time for you to consider what you need in order to stay committed to this renewed relationship with God, with your husband or wife, and with your family. Consider the factors that put you at risk of relapse and circumstances that may compromise your sexual or moral sobriety. Do not leave it to God to magically protect you. Allow God's Spirit to help you devise and plan specific strategies to guard and protect you.

Move in a Constant Direction

If you are lost in the wilderness, your survival may depend on whether you are walking in circles or proceeding in one constant direction. Choose one direction to go—north, south, east, or west—and stay in that direction. Whether following the sun that rises in the east and sets in the west, or moss growing on the north side of trees, or the North Star by night, continue to travel in that direction until you find your way out. Of course, if you have a compass, use it!

If you are lost in the wilderness of cybersex and Internet pornography, set your spiritual direction to move constantly toward God. Avoid paths that may divert or distract you from returning to that relationship. Scripture serves as a compass to keep you on that path. We suggest that you design a schedule of regular Bible reading, especially during those times when you were tempted to use pornography. At times of greatest weakness, God's Word will help keep you on the path of redemption.

Continually Scan the Horizon

Those who are lost in the wilderness know intuitively to scan the horizon for signs of civilization. Especially in the dark of night, the discovery of lights in the distance is a heartening indication that shelter and aid will soon be available.

For those who are lost in the darkness of cybersex, scanning the horizon means actively searching for resources to assist you. In relationships and marriages where one or both partners struggle with some aspect of the relationship, it is often wise to seek out counsel from other Christians. This can include pastoral guidance or professional counseling.

Mary needed to communicate to her husband her loneliness and her need for affection that was going unmet. The two of them needed to talk openly about their marriage in order to repair the trust and bond that had been damaged.

Sometimes couples struggle with this type of communication. In cases where anger and tension are so strong that it feels unsafe to express themselves openly, a counselor can help them break this impasse.

Don't let pride or embarrassment get in the way of seeking the resources that are available. Counselors are trained to help people who are stuck. They can shed light on problems and offer solutions, and you can be certain that they will make an effort to help you feel more comfortable.

Questions for Reflection and Discussion

1. Why are chatrooms so dangerous for adults and children? What, if any, benefits do they offer?

2. What are some of the reasons men and women become addicted to chatrooms with sexual themes?

3. Most people realize it's a bad idea to give out personal information or meet someone in person online after meeting in a chatroom. But many of them do it anyway. What might account for this kind of behavior?

4. What are some things you could do to support a friend or family member who is addicted to chatrooms?

Chapter 7

My Deep, Dark Secret

The Destructive Cycle of Sexual Abuse

Todd's Story

Sitting on the edge of the bed, I put a single bullet into the chamber of my father's revolver. I spun the chamber and listened to each click for what felt like an eternity, until it finally stopped. With my eyes tightly closed, I raised and pressed the barrel of the gun against my temple. I cried out in despair, "Lord, let me live or let me die. My fate is in your hands." Click. The silence was deafening.

***

So how did my life reach a point of such despair that I tried to kill myself on more than one occasion?

My story begins several years ago when I was a child. In the fourth grade, I was sexually abused by a male babysitter for over a year. About once a month, my parents would go out for a night on the town. Gary was the son of my parents' best friends. They had been friends and neighbors for many years, and Gary was like a trusted member of our family. We went to the same church, and Gary was a Boy Scout. I liked Gary and always had fun when he babysat me. He was always friendly and polite and joked around in a fun way. My parents had no reason to mistrust him.

One night, Gary introduced to me to a game he called "truth or dare." He started the game by asking me to do silly things like jump up and down or make animal sounds. It was funny and we laughed a lot. We played this game every time he babysat me. One night, the game changed. We started out acting silly just like before, but as the game went on Gary dared me to touch his private parts. He told me touching his private parts was all part of the game and it would be a lot of fun. He took his penis out from under his shorts and told me to rub it for him. He told me to move my hand up and down, and he even showed me how to do it by putting his hand on top of mine. I did what he wanted me to because I was confused and too afraid to tell him no. He said I did a good job and I was winning the game. After a few minutes, Gary said the game was over. He removed my hand and put his penis back in his shorts.

Gary told me I should never tell anyone about this game because our parents would get mad and I'd get in trouble. This seemed confusing to me because I thought it was just a game, but since I didn't want to get in trouble or make Gary mad at me, I didn't tell anyone about the game. It was our little secret.

Over time, Gary's truth or dare game evolved and included much more touching than the first time we played. I touched his penis and he touched mine. It felt good when he touched mine. It sort of tickled. He told me the tickling feeling was good. He'd always tell me afterwards that the game was our secret and I'd get in trouble if I told. He also told me he'd be really mad at me if I told our secret and wouldn't play with me anymore. He said his parents would be so mad that I wouldn't be allowed to go swimming in their swimming pool. So I kept my promise. The secret was safe with me.

As Gary's game evolved over the course of a year, my feelings about the game changed. It wasn't fun anymore. I felt like something was wrong, but I wasn't sure what to do about it, and I didn't want to get in trouble. All Gary wanted to do when he babysat me was play that stupid game. Gary was sexually abusing me, but I didn't know that then. It was rather traumatic to me; I'll skip the grizzly details. It's still unpleasant to talk about it to this day. I never told my parents of the abuse until I got in trouble with the law. I'll talk more about that later.

* * *

The secret I kept burned inside of me for a very long time, but, like many victims of abuse, I was too ashamed and embarrassed to talk openly about it. I was also a little afraid of Gary. He told me never to tell of our game, and since he was older than me, I listened. I also thought that if I kept it secret, the bad feelings I had would somehow go away over time. Gary and his family eventually moved away, so the abuse stopped. I missed Gary, but I was glad we didn't have to play the game anymore. I tried to forget about it, but I couldn't get it out of my head. I wanted to tell someone but was still afraid Gary would find out and I would get in trouble.

To this day, I'm not totally sure why I didn't tell my parents when I suspected something was wrong. I think they would have believed me, but something kept me from telling the secret. Maybe I believed my parents would be mad and blame me for what had happened. I also didn't want to lose

141

Gary's friendship or not be allowed to swim in his pool. For a long time I believed I'd done something wrong and shouldn't have let Gary touch me. I felt I was to blame for not making him stop.

During my teenage years, I struggled with many issues that I now believe are directly connected to my abuse. I was often depressed, but I put on a mask and tried to act like everything was OK. I had some friends, but it was hard to let anyone get close to me. I was afraid they would somehow find out about the abuse and stop liking me.

I tried hard not to think about it, but this became more difficult when I reached puberty. I liked girls, but a part of me secretly worried that I might be gay. I didn't have sexual feelings for guys so I told myself I must not be. But in the back of my mind, I always worried about it. I worried that if my peers found out I had been abused by a guy, they would think I was gay. I wanted to be invisible. I've learned that this is a common worry for boys who've been abused by males. I felt so alone. I wondered what was wrong with me, but there was no way I was going to openly talk about this with anyone. I worried that if I opened up just a little, someone would figure out I'd been abused.

As I became more depressed, I felt like staying home more than going out with friends. I didn't go to football or basketball games like other kids my age. Home felt much safer than the social world of school. I was tired a lot and sometimes sad without knowing why. My social confidence was in the pits. I knew I was missing out on life, but I really didn't care. The more socially isolated I became, the more depressed I felt. It was a vicious cycle that I didn't know how to break.

The only friends I had at the time were two cousins who introduced me to video games. I quickly became hooked on them because I could play by myself and safely retreat from the real world. Before long, I told my parents I needed a computer for school. I think they agreed because they hoped it would make me happy.

I quickly learned the ins and outs of computers, including the Internet. One day while working on a homework assignment, I went to a website I thought would be appropriate for the topic I was researching. To my amazement, pictures of hot-looking naked women popped up! I was excited by what I saw. I followed the link for a free tour of the site. Wow, more pictures!

I became addicted to pornography overnight. I never spent any money buying porn pictures and I didn't need to—they were all free. I became so obsessed over time that I would keep my computer running all day, downloading as many pictures as I could. I collected thousands of images every day, far too many to ever look at. So I'd save them onto discs.

Most nights I'd look at the pictures and masturbate. It made me feel good, at least temporarily. Sometimes I'd sit at the computer for hours, getting aroused, but holding off my orgasm until I found just the right picture that pushed me over the edge. It was like I was in a trance, losing all perspective of time.

I kept my door locked so my parents wouldn't walk in on me. Sometimes they'd ask what I was doing all night in my room with the door locked. I'd just lie and say I was doing a school project and needed privacy. They had no clue what I was really up to. If by chance they would walk in on me, I knew how to change the computer screen really fast and hide the pornography. I'd sometimes get mad at them and even yell at them if they interrupted me. It was like they were spoiling my private time.

I continued to go to school but didn't have many friends. My grades really suffered, and I lost interest in school altogether. I spent most of the time daydreaming about the pornography I'd be viewing when I got home.

I thought about my sexual abuse often, but still kept it secret. My self-esteem was low. I felt trapped. There were times I thought about hanging myself or shooting myself. The depth of my pain was too much to bear most of the time. Even though masturbation and pornography gave me some temporary relief, the problems were always there. The more depressed and isolated I became, the more I escaped to my computer. I could control the computer. I couldn't control people.

One day while online, my cousin instant-messaged me. He suggested I contact this girl he'd met online. (I'll call her Shayla, not her real name.) I sent her an instant message, and she responded right away. It was so cool. We chatted for a little bit, nothing too serious. Over the next few weeks, we struck up a friendship and shared more about ourselves.

Shayla lived with her parents, who argued and fought a lot, and she was very unhappy and depressed, just like me. I also found out that she was younger than me—a minor in fact. But I didn't dwell on that too much. A girl was talking to me, taking interest in me even! Who cared how old she was?

She even shared with me that she'd been abused. I felt reassured that there was someone out there like me, someone who could relate to me.

I finally got up the courage and told her I'd been sexually abused when I was younger, and she was very understanding. She didn't make fun of me or reject me. She had a way about her that made me feel truly understood.

I noticed my feelings for Shayla starting to grow. I had another reason for looking forward to coming home from school now. I hoped she'd be online so we could chat, but I never told her about my pornography problem. I didn't want to risk scaring her away. It's funny how I could tell her about my abuse, but not about my use of pornography. Maybe I didn't realize how serious my problem was at the time I met her, even though collecting porn pictures had become as much a part of my daily life as brushing my teeth. I didn't want to reveal that part of myself. I was still keeping secrets.

One day Shayla suggested we send each other pictures of ourselves. I was excited about seeing what she looked like, yet nervous that she would think I was ugly and reject me. I knew in the back of my mind that she was a minor. But I was so needy for a friend that I didn't want her age to matter.

We each had digital cameras, so we took pictures and sent them to each other. She was so cute, I couldn't believe it. But the next day she wasn't online. My worst fear was confirmed: she thought I was ugly and didn't want to chat anymore. I was instantly depressed and felt sick to my stomach. I told my parents I had the flu and stayed home from school the next day.

I did nothing but lie around feeling depressed. Later in the day, when I knew Shayla was home from school, I got on the computer to see if she was online. She was. I wanted to send her an instant message, but I was afraid she would ignore me. I sat there, just staring at the computer screen. And then, she sent me a message. A friendly message. She apologized for not being online the previous day. We started to chat again. I was euphoric. She still liked me.

As time went on, I suggested we send naked pictures of ourselves to each other. To my delighted surprise, Shayla agreed. That was such a rush. I started to think of her as my girlfriend. Even though I didn't really know her, I thought I did. Her sending pictures to me made me feel she really cared for me. Sometimes I masturbated to her naked pictures. I never told her that. But doing so made me feel closer to her.

One day, she suggested we talk on the phone and even meet each other. She lived in another state, so meeting didn't seem that practical, but I called her. Her voice was so cute. I was falling in love. Finally, a girl who liked me! I didn't care that she was a lot younger. She made me feel good about myself. That's all that mattered.

We arranged to meet. I was going to skip school, borrow my parents' car, and drive the three hours to meet her. I couldn't sleep the entire week. Thoughts of Shayla and the sex we might have consumed me.

As I was driving to meet her, though, I was tempted to turn around and go home. A voice in my head kept telling me this was wrong and I could get in trouble. But it was too late. I had to see in person the girl of my dreams.

We'd planned to meet in a hotel room in a not-so-good part of town. I got lost a few times, but finally found the hotel. After parking the car, I took a deep breath and knocked on the door. The door opened, and I was tackled by three police officers who forced my hands behind my back and handcuffed them. They put me in a police car and drove me to jail. I was shaking all over and felt like I wanted to cry. It was the worst moment of my life.

I never did meet Shayla. I later learned she was scared of meeting me and told one of her girlfriends about our plans. Her girlfriend told her parents, who then called the police.

I was allowed to make one phone call from jail. That was the hardest phone call I ever made to my parents. I stuttered at first, but finally told my mother what happened. She cried a lot. I then told my dad. He was quiet. That meant he was too angry to say anything. I'd let both my parents down. I just wanted them to tell me everything would be OK. I felt so utterly alone.

The police were not supportive. I could tell they thought I was a bad person by the way they treated me and talked to me. They thought I meant to harm Shayla, which was so not true. But they didn't believe me and made me feel like such a loser. They fingerprinted me and took my picture. They told me I was being arrested and advised me to call an attorney. Who could I call? I didn't know any attorneys. I had never gotten in trouble before. I didn't know what to do. I waited for my parents to come and see me. That was longest wait of my life. I was put in a holding cell with some scary men who looked like hardened criminals.

After my parents posted bail, I was allowed to go home with them. The ride home was silent. I didn't know what to say. I was ashamed and embarrassed. I just wanted to close my eyes and make it all go away. It didn't go away, though; it was just the beginning of a long and frightening ordeal.

My parents found an attorney for me. He explained how much trouble I could be in. I didn't really understand all the legal words he used, so I kept quiet. My parents did the talking for me. The first recommendation he made was to call a counselor he had worked with and trusted. My parents called the counselor and set up the first session for me. I was so scared to go to counseling. As it turned out, this is the best advice I was ever given. It took time to trust my counselor, but when I did, I told him my life story.

What I learned from counseling was that the actions that got me into trouble with the law stemmed from my past sexual abuse. That doesn't excuse my behavior, but it helped me to understand why I did what I did. For years I'd tried to cover up the abuse and mask my feelings, but I paid a high price. It doesn't really seem fair that I had to suffer so much. I lost perspective on reality. I used the computer to hide behind and to create what I thought was a safe haven in the privacy of my bedroom. My emotional pain made me feel vulnerable, so I turned to the computer and pornography to escape reality. I created a fantasy world.

I saw and experienced the dark side of online pornography first-hand. The use of pornography made me more depressed. It allowed me to maintain my denial about my own abuse. Then, when Shayla began showing an interest in me, I fantasized that she was my girlfriend—and we'd never even met before! But she filled the need I had for companionship. After I lost her, I was sad for a very long time.

I haven't talked with Shayla since the day of my arrest. I got rid of all my Internet pornography. Every last picture. I never want to go back to that darkness again.

Since then, I've finished high school and college. I joined a young adult Bible study. I still get depressed now and then, but I don't think about suicide anymore. I know it will take time to completely get over my depression. I haven't looked at pornography in a long time. I'm on my way to recovery. And I've even found a girlfriend who's my age.

Now I tell anyone who's been a victim of childhood abuse that it's important to talk about it and understand how it can affect you. I also tell anyone who will listen to stay away from online pornography. It nearly ruined my life. Thank God, I'm free.

The Impact of Child Sexual Abuse

The destructive cycle of child abuse affects many people. Sexual abuse happens to both boys and girls of all ages. It takes a lot of courage for a child to disclose the abuse. Some victims of child abuse tell a trusted adult right away. This is a good thing, and in most cases it stops the abuse from continuing. But many children are so confused, frightened, and ashamed that they keep the abuse secret for years— sometimes for a whole lifetime—while suffering in silence.

Often offenders, like the one in Todd's story, use threats to scare children into keeping the abuse a secret. They tell children they will get into trouble or go to jail if caught. Or that their mother will be angry and the abuse will lead to divorce. They may convince the child that no adult will believe them. In some cases, offenders are very clever in making the child feel as if he or she desired the abuse. When this happens, the child feels guilty and hides the secret even from trusted adults or peers. Whatever the reason, children are often conflicted about reporting abuse. They know or have a sense the abuse is wrong, but it's just too hard to tell someone about it.

Sexual abuse damages children's self-esteem and self-worth. They feel dirty. They feel the pain of betrayal by a trusted adult. Sometimes children are abused by older children in their neighborhood or by a relative or someone else the family trusts, such as a babysitter. The victim may feel emotionally close to the offender, like a father figure. If that's the case, children are torn between reporting the abuse and possibly breaking up their family, not to mention hurting the offender's feelings. They may take a protective role, actually taking care of the offender's emotional needs.

Regardless of the type of abuse or the relationship between victim and offender, abuse can have long-term emotional effects. Those who have been abused as children may struggle with trust and intimacy in adult relationships, even in marriage. Some victims hate sex because it triggers old feelings of abuse. It's difficult for them to enjoy the physical aspect of marriage. They feel inhibited and have a hard time trusting their partner and letting go of the past. They fear sexual pleasure because it makes them feel guilty and ashamed. It can be like reliving the abuse all over again.

Other victims react quite differently. They may develop a pattern of sexual promiscuity, using sex as a way to get attention and affection. They are confused about true love and intimacy. Although they want love and affection, they try to get it the wrong way. If they are unaware that their sexual behavior is related to their past abuse, they may repeat the pattern of jumping in and out of sexual relationships over and over again, losing their self-respect along the way.

Sexual abuse affects people in different ways. Todd's history of childhood sexual abuse played a major role in the development of his addiction to pornography. Despite a loving family, he kept his dark secret for a very long time. Abuse traumatized him and affected his psychological development in a negative way. Not all victims of abuse engage in self-destructive patterns. Some manage to survive their ordeal without traumatic consequences such as depression and suicide. But for many, the impact of abuse is devastating and life-changing.

Todd became depressed and suicidal. He felt ashamed. He was fearful of his parents' reaction if he disclosed the truth and fearful of the offender's reaction. Todd blamed himself for the abuse, even though he was only a child and it wasn't his fault. He developed low self-esteem. With that came feelings of insecurity and inadequacy as a male, as well as social anxiety among his peers. All these dynamics made him fragile and vulnerable to the use of pornography. The computer and the Internet became Todd's refuge, a temporary way to escape his inner pain. The more he withdrew from healthy social relationships, the more he depended on the Internet.

When Todd discovered pornography, he was immediately aroused and excited. One picture led to two pictures and then more. Over time, he became addicted to pornography. He felt ashamed of this behavior, but because he was so lonely most of the time, he began to justify his actions. This justification led to more use, and he found himself trapped in a dark world. The more time he spent trying to find pleasure through sexual arousal, the more depressed he became. The more depressed he became, the more he withdrew from healthy relationships. He became a loner. His use of pornography escalated. It was a vicious cycle from which he could not escape.

When Todd first talked to a girl online, even though she was a minor, he felt a sense of social connection he was not able to achieve at school or through other types of social activities. The computer provided a barrier of safety. He didn't have to worry about rejection based on physical appearance. He was talking to someone and she was actually talking back!

Given his neediness, this type of virtual interaction made him feel better. He began to look forward to talking with this girl every day. That's all he thought about at school. He wanted to get home as fast as he could to check his e-mail. He chatted with her into the late hours of the night. His schoolwork suffered. He was tired a lot. He lied to his parents, telling them he was up late working on school projects. Despite knowing this girl was a minor, he began to care for her. And as she shared personal information, he believed she cared for him. Although he had never seen her, he began to form a mental picture of her and became attracted to her.

In the back of Todd's mind he knew she might not be the girl of his dreams, but his need for social connection was so strong that he tried to block this from his mind. As his confidence in the relationship grew, exchanging pictures over the Internet fueled Todd's desire for her. He began to obsess about her and to dream of a future together. Once his fear of rejection subsided, they exchanged more pictures. This was a big moment for Todd. She still liked him even when she'd seen his picture. He cherished the pictures she sent him, taping her photo to his computer monitor every time he talked with her.

Exchanging pictures led to the next step of wanting to hear her voice and chat on the phone. She gave Todd her phone number, and he called her. Once they were comfortable talking on the phone, the desire to meet and see each other was the next natural step. The more he fantasized about her as their relationship developed, the less Todd thought about her being a minor. His desire for affection and attention was stronger than his concern about any social or legal consequences. Once Todd decided to meet her, he blocked out any fear of consequences. He'd found someone with whom he could bond emotionally.

When Todd was arrested by the police, his fantasy world came crashing down. He was scared to death. He really meant no harm to this girl. From his childhood abuse to his addiction to pornography, Todd's life had been spiraling downward for a very long time. Getting caught was actually a blessing in disguise. It led him to counseling, which, in turn, led to disclosing the abuse to his parents and confronting his offender face to face, and, eventually, to developing social confidence and self-esteem.

Todd has made great strides in his personal growth. He has broken the bonds of addiction to pornography. He completed college, found a job, and developed a steady relationship with a girl his own age. In the end, Todd's is a story of hope and renewal. The healing process takes time, but it's possible to overcome the impact of childhood sexual abuse. The road may be challenging, but many have the courage to cross the finish line. And many resources are available to help those who have been abused find their way toward healing and wholeness.

A Pastor's Perspective

During a men's Bible study, Todd disclosed that he was a victim of sexual abuse. At first I wasn't sure what to say. I didn't want to say the wrong thing. I prayed for guidance and was moved to show Todd love and support. He had been keeping his secret for a long time. Todd felt that God had abandoned him when he was a child. Todd was embarrassed to talk about it, but I reassured him of God's love and kindness and told him he could trust God to be with him always.

Over time I've seen Todd's faith grow and mature. He has made significant strides in healing. In the near future, Todd will be leading a men's group.

Common Effects of Untreated Sexual Abuse

As we've already noted, sexual abuse affects victims in different ways. Some recover rapidly and go on to live healthy and productive lives. For others, however, untreated symptoms of abuse persist into adulthood. According to The National Center for Post Traumatic Stress Disorders[1], victims of abuse frequently experience the following problems:

- Post-traumatic stress disorder or anxiety

- Depression and thoughts of suicide

- Sexual anxiety and disorders

- Poor body image and low self-esteem

- Unhealthy behaviors, such as alcohol abuse, drug abuse, self-mutilation, or binging and purging

Warning Signs of Child Sexual Abuse

No parent likes to think about sexual abuse. But the world has become an increasingly dangerous place for children. We want to protect our children and keep them safe. Knowing the common warning signs of sexual abuse can help you keep kids safe.

The Safe Child Program[2] defines sexual abuse as follows:

> any sexual contact with a child or the use of a child for the sexual pleasure of someone else. This may include exposing private parts to the child or asking the child to expose him or herself, fondling of the genitals or requests for the child to do so, oral sex or attempts to enter the vagina or anus with fingers, objects or penis, although actual penetration is rarely achieved.

There are a number of warning signs that a child may have been sexually abused. These include physical and behavioral indicators.

Physical indicators include the following:

- Difficulty walking or sitting
- Torn clothing
- Stained or bloody underwear
- Pain or itching in genital area
- Venereal disease, especially in preteens
- Pregnancy

Behavioral indicators include the following:

- Inappropriate displays of affection
- Discomfort with or rejection of typical family affection
- Sleep problems, including insomnia, nightmares, refusal to sleep alone, or suddenly insisting on a night light

Common Fears about Reporting Abuse

There are many reasons why victims of sexual abuse keep it a secret. The following are some of the most common reasons shared by male and female victims during counseling:

- It's my fault.
- I'll get into some type of trouble.
- No one will believe me.
- My mom will be mad when he (dad or stepdad) leaves.
- I'm confused; I don't know what to do.
- I feel ashamed and guilty.
- The offender might go to jail, and I still care about him.
- He won't like me anymore.
- He said he'd hurt me or someone in my family if I tell.
- I don't want to have to tell this story to strangers over and over again.
- I'm scared.
- I didn't make it stop.
- I'm too depressed to talk about it.
- I don't want to think about it. I'm trying to block it out of my mind.
- Kids at school will find out.
- They will call me gay.
- I'm afraid I'll have to testify in court.
- My parents won't trust me to go anywhere on my own again.
- My friends might shun me, hate me, or spread rumors about me.

- Regressive behaviors, including thumb-sucking, bed-wetting, infantile behaviors, or other signs of dependency

- Extreme clinginess or other signs of fearfulness

- An unwillingness to participate in or reluctance to change clothing for gym class

- Bizarre or unusual sophistication pertaining to sexual behavior or knowledge, including sexual acting out
- Reports of sexual assault by a parent or guardian
- Sudden changes in behavior or school performance
- Learning problems (or difficulty concentrating) that cannot be attributed to specific physical or psychological causes
- Watchfulness, as if preparing for something bad to happen
- Unusual compliance, passivity, or withdrawal
- A pattern of arriving early to activities, staying late, and not wanting to go home
- Noticeable fear of a particular person or certain places
- Unusual or unexpected response from the child when questioned about being touched by someone
- Unreasonable fear of a physical exam
- Drawings depicting sexual acts
- A sudden awareness of genitals and sexual acts and words
- Attempts to get other children to perform sexual acts

Scriptural Guidance for Those in the Depths of Despair

In the story that introduced this chapter, Todd was so distraught with his circumstances that he seriously considered suicide. For Todd and others who experience this depth of despair, these words from the Old Testament may be particularly helpful:

Now Ahab told Jezebel everything Elijah had done and how he had killed all the prophets with the sword. So Jezebel sent a messenger to Elijah to say, "May the gods deal with me, be it ever so severely, if by this time tomorrow I do not make your life like that of one of them."

Statistics[3]

- One in four girls is sexually abused before the age of eighteen.
- One in six boys is sexually abused before the age of eighteen.
- One in five children is solicited sexually while on the Internet.
- An estimated 39 million survivors of childhood sexual abuse exist in America today.
- Thirty to forty percent of victims are abused by a family member.
- Another 50 percent are abused by someone outside of the family whom they know and trust.
- Approximately 40 percent are abused by older or larger children whom they know.
- Only 10 percent of abuse victims are abused by strangers.
- The median age for reported abuse is nine years old.
- More than 20 percent of children are sexually abused before the age of eight.
- Almost 80 percent initially deny abuse or are tentative in disclosing. Of those who do disclose, approximately 75 percent disclose accidentally. Additionally, of those who do disclose, more than 20 percent eventually recant even though the abuse occurred.
- Fabricated sexual abuse reports constitute only 1 to 4 percent of all reported cases. Of these reports, 75 percent are falsely reported by adults and 25 percent are reported by children. Children only fabricate ½ percent of the time.

Elijah was afraid and ran for his life. When he came to Beersheba in Judah, he left his servant there, while he himself went a day's journey into the wilderness. He came to a broom bush, sat down under it and prayed that he might die. "I have had enough, Lord," he said. "Take my life; I am no better than my ancestors." Then he lay down under the tree and fell asleep.

All at once an angel touched him and said, "Get up and eat." He looked around, and there by his head was some bread baked over hot coals, and a jar of water. He ate and drank and then lay down again.

The angel of the Lord came back a second time and touched him and said, "Get up and eat, for the journey is too much for you." So he got up and ate and drank. Strengthened by that food, he traveled forty days and forty nights until he reached Horeb, the mountain of God. There he went into a cave and spent the night.

And the word of the Lord came to him: "What are you doing here, Elijah?"

He replied, "I have been very zealous for the Lord God Almighty. The Israelites have rejected your covenant, torn down your altars, and put your prophets to death with the sword. I am the only one left, and now they are trying to kill me too."

The Lord said, "Go out and stand on the mountain in the presence of the Lord, for the Lord is about to pass by."

Then a great and powerful wind tore the mountains apart and shattered the rocks before the Lord, but the Lord was not in the wind. After the wind there was an earthquake, but the Lord was not in the earthquake. After the earthquake came a fire, but the Lord was not in the fire. And after the fire came a gentle whisper. When

Elijah heard it, he pulled his cloak over his face and went out and stood at the mouth of the cave.

Then a voice said to him, "What are you doing here, Elijah?"

He replied, "I have been very zealous for the Lord God Almighty. The Israelites have rejected your covenant, torn down your altars, and put your prophets to death with the sword. I am the only one left, and now they are trying to kill me too."

The Lord said to him, "Go back the way you came, and go to the Desert of Damascus."

—1 Kings 19:1-15

This story about Elijah is not just a Scripture passage that tells of bit of prophetic history. This is a story that tells us how to see the light of God when we are in our darkest moments. Elijah knew hopelessness; he knew what it is to face a river of despair. He was so low that he prayed for his own death: "I have had enough, Lord. Take my life."

The day before, Elijah had been anything but depressed. He had been on Mount Carmel, performing a miracle that demonstrated the power of God. Soon after, he ordered the slaughter of the pagan "prophets of Baal."

These "prophets of Baal" belonged to Queen Jezebel, who was enraged when she found out what Elijah had done. She sent a messenger to inform Elijah that she had every intention of hunting him down to kill him.

Elijah fled into the desert, running for his life. But his desert wasn't just a barren piece of land, his wilderness was emotional and spiritual as well. For it was there that he found himself sitting under a tree praying, "I have had enough, Lord. Take my life."

As he lay down under the tree and fell asleep, an angel touched him and said, "Get up and eat." In the midst of his wilderness experience, Elijah experienced the sustaining power of God's presence. In the depths of his despair, the prophet encounters grace.

By all outward appearances, Christians who have unresolved issues stemming from childhood sexual abuse and who, as adults, are caught up in the cycle of addiction to Internet pornography, may be good, Christian people, devoted to their faith. Some are considered to be pillars of the Christian community. But they bear the burden of hiding a dark secret behind the closed doors of their private lives. When their behavior is exposed and they are confronted by the reality of their past abuse, many of them ask, "How will I ever have the strength to face it?" Overwhelmed with embarrassment and shame, fear, and anxiety, they wonder how they can find the strength to survive. Some, like Todd, succumb to despair and contemplate suicide.

But there is hope. In the midst of Elijah's crisis, God sent an angel. And to those whose lives are in crisis because of cybersexual behavior and a history of sexual abuse, God also sends his angels.

In both Hebrew and Greek, the languages of the Old and New Testaments, the word for angel is "messenger." References to God's messengers are sprinkled throughout the Bible. The strangers who appeared at Abraham and Sarah's tent to tell her she would bear a son in her old age were angels (messengers) from God. The messenger who told the virgin Mary that she would conceive a child was the angel Gabriel. Soon after, the shepherds watching over their flocks by night were visited by divine messengers. And on Easter morning, an angel delivered the message of Jesus' resurrection at the empty tomb.

The message of the Bible is clear: keep your eyes open for "angels unaware." For those in the depths of despair, the question is: Are there angels in your life? Can you see God's messengers operating in and through your life? Are you paying enough attention to see them?

Perhaps God is using you as a messenger of grace. Perhaps you will be used to provide comfort to someone in despair, like the angel who ministered to Elijah beneath his tree. Perhaps you'll bring a message of hope to a friend as she struggles with past trauma. Or perhaps God is using you as a guardian angel, helping to protect a loved one from the dangers of the Internet.

Up on Mount Horeb, the angel of the Lord provided food and water for Elijah. And whether we are God's angels ministering to those who struggle, or whether we are the ones being ministered unto, the grace of God provides us not just with bread but the bread of life; not just with water but the living water of Christ. As Jesus said, "Those who drink the water I give them will never thirst" (John 4:13).

Renewal and Restoration: The Process Begins

For victims of abuse, the first step in recovery is to admit the abuse and pray for healing. Trying to block out or forget the abuse actually makes it worse; you need to deal with it directly. Christians have an advantage when dealing with abuse: God understands and helps heal the inner pain.

When Todd finally broke the code of silence, he took a very important step toward healing. Of course he was afraid: afraid of awakening old and bad feelings related to the abuse that he had tried to silence by keeping them secret. But by confronting the abuse, he began to empower himself. No longer would he allow fear rule him. Sometimes talking about abuse is like reliving it emotionally. It hurts. Some people cry. Some get very angry. These are all normal feelings and reactions, and experiencing them is a step toward health. Taking this path helps lessen the powerful grip of negative feelings and emotions, the ones kept repressed or denied. It may hurt at first, but over time, people start to feel better after releasing the emotions that have been trapped for so long.

The first person Todd disclosed his abuse to was his counselor. This occurred once he determined the counselor to be a safe person. Since Todd had been abused by a male, it took time for him to trust his male counselor. This betrayal of trust was a key dynamic in becoming a victim of abuse. Taking the risk of rebuilding trust with someone was an important step. Todd had a desire to be understood and not shamed for his past. When his confidence grew, he took another important step toward healing. He told his mother and father about the abuse. They were supportive and nonjudgmental. When his fears of rejection and shame did not come true, his progress in rebuilding trust took another step forward.

Gradually Todd began to understand how abuse had affected his life. He came to realize that the abuse was a major factor in his history of depression and social anxiety, and specifically recognized how it affected his desire for pornography. He began to take steps to improve his self-esteem and social confidence. This process took time. It's important to note that there are no hard and fast rules on how long the healing process should take. Each person approaches healing at his or her own pace.

Abuse sometimes damages a person's ability to believe in and trust God. We call this spiritual abuse. It's hard to trust an authority figure like God when one has been traumatized by an authority figure, especially if that person is a proclaimed Christian. For years Todd was angry with God. He thought God should have intervened and protected him from the abuse. The resulting problems he experienced led him to conclude that God had abandoned him and must have hated him. For a long time, Todd was too angry and ashamed to talk with God. During the dark days of his depression and sexual acting out, Todd tempted God by driving too fast with his eyes closed for a few seconds. He repeated this deadly game day after day.

One day while driving, Todd hit a patch of ice and slid off the road into the ditch. Todd was scared, but no one was hurt. A kind elderly person came to his rescue. This made an impression on Todd. Someone had reached out to him in his time of need. Todd says he'll never forget that moment. He recognized it as a wake-up call, and he never played this game again.

Looking back, Todd realizes that even though he was so low and depressed that he engaged in this reckless behavior, he didn't really want to die. He wanted to be rescued. He wanted to be set free from his inner turmoil and the years of pain that had imprisoned him.

Todd continues to make progress in his life. Still in counseling, he is active in his church and hopes to marry. By breaking his silence, Todd was able to break the cycle of abuse that almost cost him his life—physically, emotionally, and spiritually. By disclosing the abuse, talking about it, and understanding the impact it had on his life, Todd was able to move toward recovery and healing. No longer angry at God, he is able to trust. Although he has tried to forgive his offender, this will take more time.

If you are a victim of any type of abuse—sexual, physical, emotional, or spiritual—know that you are not alone. Many people have shared that same wilderness experience. Todd found a spiritual path that led him out of the wilderness of despair. You can be sure that God will give you what you need to take this journey as well. By God's grace and with the help of his messengers, renewal and restoration are available to all, one step at a time.

Strategies for Renewal

Admitting one's abuse, talking about it, and understanding its effects are the hallmarks of abuse recovery. This leads to empowerment and hope. The following strategies are designed to help victims identify and express their feelings about the abuse and their abuser.

A Letter Destroyed

Write a letter to your offender, but don't send it. Write down all your thoughts and feelings. Say whatever you want to say. You are no longer a victim. You have the power, control, and right to express yourself however you wish to—it's your letter. The offender will never read or see it, so you can be as free as you want in your expression. Talk about your anger. Talk about your hurt. Talk about how the abuse has affected you. If you want the offender to go to jail or prison, say so. Don't hold back. Give yourself permission to tell it like it is. These are your feelings. Maybe you've never been able to tell your offender exactly how you feel—this is your opportunity. Writing your feelings down is a safe way to express yourself. In addition, it is an effective way to organize your thoughts and feelings about the offense.

Hold onto the letter for a day or two or for as long as you want. Then rip it up. Get rid of it. This is a symbolic gesture that the abuse is over, and you are no longer held captive to it. This exercise is especially helpful to those who are still struggling with some aspect of abuse.

A Letter Sent

This intervention is very similar to the one above. But because it's more confrontational, some victims feel uncomfortable taking this step. It's riskier. The offender may get angry, or he or she may be understanding and contrite. People who take this step are often more careful with what they say and how they say it. They are more restrained. You need to decide what's right for you. If sending a letter feels uncomfortable or unsafe, then it's best not to send it.

A Phone Call

Talking to he offender on the phone is a more direct form of communication. Some may prefer this approach, while others may feel too intimidated or do not want to hear the offender's voice. Again, it's not possible to predict how the offender will react. Some people who take this step write down what they want to say because it's easier. The bottom line is, if you feel unsafe or highly anxious, this step is probably not for you.

Face-to-Face Contact

This step involves talking to the offender directly. Most victims pick a place to meet where they feel safe—perhaps a public place. Some take a support person along to either sit in on the conversation or wait in the car. Safety is always the first priority. It's difficult to talk to an offender directly about abuse. Usually it should only be done after the victim has gone through counseling, and the counselor has helped prepare the victim for such an encounter.

An Invitation to Counseling

Inviting an offender to participate in counseling can be a very rewarding and healing experience. Be aware, however, that most offenders are resistant to this invitation. In most cases, the counselor helps establish safety within the confines of the therapy office and decides with the victim the purpose and goals of the session. The offender is typically invited by the victim to attend a counseling session. This can occur by way of a letter or a phone call, which may take place from the counselor's office. The counselor could also play a role in constructing the letter. Even if the invitation is rejected, this step is a form of empowerment. The courage required to make this invitation is a sign that healing is taking place.

A Word from Todd's Mom

When my husband and I first found out Todd had been arrested, we were shocked. We had not raised our son to get in trouble with the law. We were hurt, angry, confused, sad, and scared. We knew Todd had always struggled socially, but we hoped he would grow out of it. We had no clue he had been sexually abused.

I cried for days when he first told us. I couldn't sleep, and I kept picturing him getting abused. This all seemed like a bad dream. We could not understand why he never told us what happened. I couldn't fathom how it had happened right under my nose. Moreover, I couldn't understand why anyone would want to hurt my son like that.

I did not realize how frightened he was of his offender and how his fear and shame affected him so deeply. I also had no clue about the dangers of the Internet, especially all the pornography out there. It is very frightening to think how many kids are involved in this type of problem without parents knowing what's going on.

I'm glad Todd's secret about his abusive past and pornography addiction is now out in the open. He went to counseling and has made a lot of progress. I know it's been a painful process for him—and for us as well—but he's done a lot of growing up over the past few years. He had strayed from church, but now attends regularly. And his girlfriend seems really nice and supportive of him. Suicidal thinking, abuse, addiction, and legal trouble are a parent's worst nightmare. But now there is hope where there once was despair. That's something to be thankful for.

A Word from Todd's Counselor

Todd was referred to me for counseling by his attorney. I've worked with Todd for over three years and have gotten to know him quite well. At the onset of counseling, Todd was quiet and soft-spoken. It was difficult for him to talk openly about his thoughts and feelings. He was very suspicious and mistrustful. He suffered from low self-esteem and self-confidence. It was obvious Todd did not like himself very much. As Todd began to trust me more, he felt safe enough to share his life story. This was both a painful yet rewarding journey of self-discovery.

Todd revealed he had a secret he'd safeguarded for years—he had been sexually abused by a babysitter when he was a child. Over a period of months, he shared only what he felt comfortable sharing during any given session. He described in vivid detail how he was abused. He was haunted by memories he could not get out of his head. Sometimes he cried; at other times he became angry. He blamed himself and questioned why he was targeted for abuse. He was also angry with himself because he felt he should have made the abuse stop. He felt he should have been strong and tough. He felt he had done something to encourage the offender.

Todd has made significant progress in changing his view of the abuse. He now realizes that he was a child and the abuse was not his fault. This was a big therapeutic step. He still gets angry with the offender and sometimes thinks of the abuse. But he also understands that this is a normal part of the healing process.

Todd wrote a letter to his offender expressing his anger. This took months to complete. He'd kept silent for so long that he wasn't sure what to write. When he was finished, he read the letter out loud during a counseling session. After feeling some anger and crying a few tears, he ripped up the letter to symbolize he was no longer a prisoner of abuse. This action allowed him to confront his offender and let out feelings that needed to be vented. It took the power away from his abuser.

Todd is still my client. He is a fine young man, and I'm very proud of the progress he's made.

Questions for Reflection and Discussion

1. What are some of the lifelong consequences of child sexual abuse?

2. Why is it so difficult for children to share with others that they are being abused, both at the time of the abuse and even years later when they are adults? What are some common fears related to disclosing abuse?

3. What is the likely outcome for a child who tells someone he or she is being abused by a parent, friend of the family, babysitter, or stranger?

4. How can confronting an abuser, whether by letter, phone call, or in person, be "a very rewarding and healing experience"?

Chapter 8

Dancing on the Edge of a Cliff

The Legal Risk of Viewing Child Pornography

Eric's Story

Three thunderous knocks echoed through my house. I jumped up, grabbed my bathrobe, and hurried downstairs. Pulling the curtains aside, I cautiously peeked out the window. Two men dressed in dark suits stood ominously on my doorstep. I opened the door a crack as one man flashed a silver badge that read "Federal Bureau of Investigation." He asked, "Are you Mr. Smith?" With my heart pounding, I nervously nodded yes. The agent replied, "We need to talk."

* * *

I struggled for a very long time with my decision to talk about my problem with Internet pornography. I felt so much embarrassment and shame. But after considerable thought, prayer, and encouragement from a counselor, I decided to take this step and talk about it. My counselor suggested that writing my story might be therapeutic because it's a way to help others learn from my mistakes. This is my story.

My problem with pornography dates back to when I was a teenager. My father had numerous pornographic magazines hidden in his bedroom closet. I found them one day when borrowing one of his ties for church. I looked through all the pages, one by one, not wanting to miss a single picture. I was hooked immediately.

I felt sexually aroused and excited when I looked at naked people—the same type of feeling drug addicts and alcoholics experience when they get high. I got high on pornography instead of drugs. Many people may find this hard to believe, and at first I was skeptical too. I had no idea one could get addicted to pornography.

My addiction to pornographic magazines led to an addiction to pornographic movies. Prior to marriage, I had a collection of movies and magazines. When I got married, I knew pornography should not be a part of a Christian home so I got rid of them. Despite this, my craving for pornography did not subside. My struggle to control these cravings was a tough battle. I prayed for change and spiritual renewal, and there were times when I'd go without pornography for weeks and even months. I'd feel a sense of confidence that I was in control of this evil, but then the feelings and urges to use would return.

There were many times I didn't even care about stopping the craving to use again. The feelings were so strong I just couldn't help myself. I'd tell myself I wasn't really hurting anyone; there were people who did worse things than I was doing. After all, I was a good provider, I worked on my marriage, and most people probably thought I was a good parent as well. I never cheated on my wife—unless you count the pornography.

What caused me to use? Sometimes I was bored with the physical aspect of my marriage. Sometimes the stress of living would get to me and I'd need a release or escape. Other times, my desire for pornography would come out of the blue and I'd have no clue what triggered it. I think it became so habitual that I didn't need a reason to use.

I continued this pattern for years, never gaining control. I just didn't know how to stop. When we bought a faster computer and hooked up to the Internet, my situation worsened. I discovered that pornography was everywhere online. I never paid for it, as most of it was free. There were pictures and pornography sites that captured any type of sexual interest or desire. I spent hours exploring, surfing one site after another. I downloaded and saved hundreds of pictures to my hard drive. I started to collect them.

My exploration of the Internet led to the discovery of chatrooms —online rooms with different titles or themes where people gather to talk about sexual themes and explore fantasies. Each room can contain as few as two people, or as many as thirty or more. You can type whatever you want in the room, or just sit back and watch others interact. The name of the room tells you the type of conversation you're likely to encounter there. Themes include "cheating on wives and husbands," "incest," "sex with children," "sex with animals"—you name it. There are even Christian-themed rooms. I visited all these rooms out of curiosity. Sometimes I chatted in the rooms, talked about one of my many fantasies, or just watched others chat about their sexual fantasies. I found it exciting and arousing.

I started to trade pictures I collected from the Internet with other males I met in chatrooms. I didn't know their ages or names.

It was called "anonymous trading." Even though free pictures were abundant online, there was something exciting about trading with others. We discussed the pictures using sexual descriptions. Some men find "trading partners"—someone to trade with on a regular basis. This is common for men who trade pictures of their wives. It's also common to trade with people who have other similar interests. For example, men who enjoy pictures of young children find men with similar interests.

There are numerous chatrooms devoted to trading pictures of young girls. The age of the girl is usually not specified because it could attract unwanted attention from the authorities, meaning the police. These girls could be in their twenties, teens, or even younger. I ventured into chatrooms with the young girl theme, and before long I put my name on something called a "list."

A list is started by someone in the chatroom. The goal is for everyone to share one picture with all group members. In return, you get a picture from everyone else on the list. It is a quick way to get pictures from others who share your interest. The person who sets up the list has software that allows him to collect and distribute the pictures to all the group members. The provider of the list instructs group members and asks who wants to be on the list. A simple response of "Yes I do" is all that is required. You send a picture from your own collection to the "list provider," who quickly distributes pictures to all the people on the list. There is no way to verify the age of anyone who chooses to participate. This means children and teenagers can get on a list and receive pornographic pictures.

Several times I received pictures in a chatroom that were of very young children. Some were totally naked, others were engaged in sexual acts with adults or other children. My first response was, "This must be wrong," and I deleted them right away. However, I kept going back to chatrooms and putting my name on lists. I kept getting pictures of young children and became more curious about them. I justified my behavior by telling myself I wasn't really hurting anyone; after all, they were just pictures. My initial concerns about the legality of what I was doing began to fade over time.

I saved several pictures on my computer of young children and started to trade these pictures with other men. I did not know these men. One day, I traded several pictures of naked young teen girls with a man I had never met before in a chatroom. That was my final trade. The next day, two agents appeared on my doorstep and I was arrested for possessing child pornography on my computer hard drive.

My arrest shocked my wife and family. I was embarrassed and ashamed. Yet that moment changed my life for the better. It was a blessing in disguise. I had to face the painful truth that I had become addicted to pornography. I had hidden the problem for a long time and was not living up to the moral standards I had set for myself and family. I had fallen from grace.

Processing through the legal system was an emotional nightmare. I had to hire an attorney, go through a psychological evaluation, seek counseling, and eventually be sentenced in court. My name and picture now appear on my state's sex offender registry. This ordeal has changed my life forever.

There are many men dancing on the edge of the cliff. Many good men flirt with disaster and potential legal consequences. I'm not a pedophile. I'm not a sexual predator. I don't think of children in sexual ways. I became addicted to online adult pornography and did not gain control of this problem until it was too late. It was never my intention to look at or download pictures of children onto my computer. I would never harm a child in any way. So here's my advice: Don't take a chance with your life. Get pornography out of your life before it's too late.

Risky Business: Dancing on the Edge of a Cliff

How does someone go from looking at and desiring adult pornography to desiring child pornography? Most people who look at child pornography should not be confused with sexual predators or pedophiles. They are not necessarily emotionally or sexually attracted to children. They have no craving or desire for children. They do not make up sexual fantasies about children.

Most people, including those who struggle with adult pornography, believe child pornography is morally wrong. So how do men like Eric get to a point where, despite knowing that child pornography is morally wrong, they look at it anyway?

Part of the problem is that child pornography is more available on the Internet than people realize. Unfortunately, it's easy to find. Websites, chatrooms, trading groups, and shareware make access to child pornography easy and tempting.

Some are curious about child pornography but are not motivated by sexual desires for children. However, if curiosity is accompanied by sexual arousal, even if the arousal is minimal at first, the risk of developing a growing desire for child pornography increases.

Looking at adult pornography puts many users in a sexually charged or aroused state, physically and mentally. If child pornography is viewed during this time, then pleasure is associated with child pornography, reinforcing the desire to look again. That pattern continues unless the individual quickly turns away from the pornography, stopping the arousal before it becomes stronger. It's a form of conditioning. Pleasure is a powerful dynamic, often causing a person to rationalize his behavior. Morals against looking at child pornography may begin to fade. What started out as curiosity begins to evolve into a pattern of desire reinforced by looking at child pornography and experiencing pleasure.

Obtaining online child pornography can lead to legal trouble in many ways, including the following:

- Trading child pornography to an undercover federal agent or police officer

- Trading child pornography to a "trustworthy" person who reports the trade to the authorities

- Purchasing online child pornographic material from undercover federal authorities

- Buying child pornography from a manufacturer or distributor who is later arrested and whose customer list is seized by the authorities

- Trading pornography on the Internet through shareware and trading groups, which can be infiltrated by the authorities

The Legal Implications of Child Pornography

The possession of child pornography is illegal. This includes pornographic pictures or movies saved or stored on a computer hard drive or onto computer discs.

Many people incorrectly assume that deleting this material after looking at it erases it from the computer. Actually the material is still saved on the computer's hard drive. The authorities have sophisticated software that can recapture these "deleted" pictures. Imagine the shock and surprise some users experience when these pictures begin showing up on their computer's monitor during an investigation. They can be used as evidence resulting in criminal charges under state and federal laws.

Frank Stanley is an experienced criminal defense lawyer in Grand Rapids, Michigan. Among other things, he specializes in the defense of individuals charged by federal or state authorities with any type of involvement with child pornography.[1] He shares his legal expertise below to help readers better understand the potential legal ramifications of possessing child pornography.

Defining the Crime

Laws governing the investigation and prosecution of child pornography vary from state to state, but looking at Michigan's law helps illustrate the point that breaking these laws is a serious matter.

In Michigan, child pornography is called "child sexually abusive material." A *child* is defined as "a person who is less than eighteen years of age." This creates an interesting anomaly in that Michigan's age of consent is sixteen. In Michigan, it would be legally permissible to have consensual sex with a sixteen-year-old but legally impermissible to photograph or record the sexual act.

The Prevalence of Child Pornography on the Internet[2]

- Demand for pornographic images of babies and toddlers on the Internet is soaring. Moreover, the images are becoming more graphically violent and disturbing.
- The typical age of children is between six and twelve, but that profile is getting younger.
- Approximately twenty new children appear on porn sites every month, many of them kidnapped or sold into the pornography industry.
- More than 20,000 images of child pornography are posted on the Internet every week.
- According to researchers who monitored the Internet over a six-week period, more than 140,000 pornographic images of children were posted. Twenty children appearing in these images were estimated to have been abused for the first time, and more than 1,000 images of each child were created.
- Child pornography generates $3 billion annually.

Child sexually abusive material is defined as "a child engaging in a listed sexual act." *A listed sexual act* is defined as "sexual intercourse, erotic fondling, sadomasochistic abuse, masturbation, passive sexual involvement, sexual excitement, or erotic nudity."

Erotic fondling is defined as "touching a person's clothed or unclothed genitals, pubic area, buttocks, or, if the person is a female, breasts, or if the person is a child, the developing or undeveloped breast area, for the purpose of real or simulated overt sexual gratification or stimulation." Physical contact that is not for the purpose of sexual gratification or stimulation is expressly excluded from the definition.

Passive sexual involvement is defined as "a real or simulated act that is designed to expose another person to or draws another person's attention to one of the listed acts for the purpose of real or simulated overt sexual gratification or stimulation."

Erotic nudity is defined as "the lascivious exhibition of genital, pubic, or rectal area of any individual." *Lascivious* is in turn defined as "wanton, lewd, lustful, and tending to produce voluptuous or lewd emotion."

Federal Law

Federal law criminalizes child pornography along with other specific crimes involving children, for example, interstate transportation of a child for an illicit purpose. Because Michigan and the federal government are two separate sovereigns, either or both jurisdictions could prosecute a person who violates the statute.

The definitional section under federal law speaks in terms of "a minor engaging in sexually explicit conduct." A *minor* is defined as "any person under the age of eighteen." However, different states may have different ages of consent for females and males.

Child pornography is defined as "any visual depiction, including any photograph, film, video, picture, or computer, or computer-generated image or picture, whether made or produced by electronic, mechanical, or other means of sexually explicit conduct."

Sexually explicit conduct is defined as including "graphic sexual intercourse of whatever type and whatever gender of the participants." This definition includes lascivious simulated sexual intercourse where the genitals, breast, or pubic area of any individual is exhibited. It also includes graphic depictions of lascivious simulated bestiality, masturbation, or sadistic or masochistic abuse and/or the graphic or simulated exhibition of the genitals or pubic area of any person.

Graphic means that "a viewer can observe any part of the genitals or pubic area of any depicted person, during any part of the time that sexually explicit conduct is being depicted."

Visual depiction is defined as including "undeveloped film and videotape, and the data stored on the computer disc or by electronic means which is capable of conversion into a visual image."

Once the authorities determine whether a picture on a computer qualifies as child pornography, a decision is made as to whether or not the individual has committed a crime. For example, Michigan identifies three tiers of conduct. Each tier is subject to a different penalty. Each requires the person to "know, have reason to know, or should be reasonably expected to know" that the depiction is a depiction of a child. A person who does not take reasonable precautions to determine the age of someone depicted can be criminally implicated even if that person did not think the image depicted a child.

Tier 1: The first tier includes anyone who "persuades, induces, entices, coerces, causes, or knowingly allows a child to engage in child sexually abusive activity for the purpose of producing any child sexually abusive material." This is commonly understood to be someone who has direct contact with the child whose images are being recorded. One published Michigan case involved one minor photographing two other minors having sex with one another.

The statute also includes in the first tier "a person who arranges for, produces, makes, or finances, or a person who attempts, prepares or conspires to arrange for, produce, make, or finance any child sexually abusive activity or child sexually abusive material."

A recent Michigan Court of Appeals case held that someone that would otherwise be a simple possessor (Tier 3) could be prosecuted as a Tier 1 violator. In that case, the individual downloaded images from the Internet onto rewritable CDs (CDRs). The CDRs were not disseminated to anyone else. They were intended as a means of storage. Nevertheless, because the individual had copied the images onto the CDRs, the court considered him to be a producer. This was deemed true even though the individual had never had contact with the child depicted and didn't know the child's identity.

Tier 2: The second tier includes a person who "distributes, promotes, or finances the distribution or promotion or receives for the purposes of distribution or promotion, or conspires, attempts, or prepares to distribute, receive, finance, or promote any child sexually abusive material." This tier has historically included individuals who disseminate the images to others and could include the original creators of the pornography. It also could include those individuals who obtain the images from whatever sources and distribute them to others. It also includes people that finance the distribution operation.

Tier 3: The third tier includes a person who knowingly possesses any child sexually abusive material. This tier has historically included the end-user, that is, an individual who possesses the material for personal reasons who had nothing to do with the original creation of the material and who does not disseminate the material to any third party.

Consequences: Federal or State Prison

Both Michigan and the federal government use sentencing guidelines to compute a sentencing range. The Michigan guidelines are presently mandatory. The federal guidelines are supposedly advisory, but they are quasi-mandatory since most sentences are imposed within those guidelines. The federal penalties are much more severe than the Michigan penalties. In a recent example, an individual who was convicted by a federal court for possession of child pornography received a fourteen-year sentence. Had that individual been prosecuted in a Michigan state court, the minimum sentence would have been approximately three years.

Numerous variables impact the type of punishment and help the authorities determine the seriousness of the consequences. For example, the age of the child, number of pornographic images involved, use of the computer, and number of victims are all examined very carefully. The likelihood of serving prison time is very real for those convicted of possession of child pornography.

This articulation of state and federal law regarding possession of child pornography should strike fear into those who have child pornography of any kind, in any form, in their possession. It's especially important to realize that deleting pictures from one's hard drive does not really delete them. Even pictures that were "deleted" years ago can be retrieved and interpreted as evidence of possessing child pornography. This is chilling news for those who believe they are protected from prosecution. And it should be a strong wake-up call for those who are experimenting with or curious about child pornography.

A Detective's View

I've investigated many cases related to child pornography. When I show up on a suspect's front step and flash my badge, the most common reaction is fear. The person reluctantly lets me in because my badge carries power and influence.

Most suspects let me inspect their computers for child pornography. If they resist, I inform them I can obtain a warrant to seize their computers by calling the authorities from their house. I always ask them if I will find something on their computers they should not have, like pictures of children. Some confess right away, while others express confidence that they don't have anything illegal.

As I check out their computers using special software and pictures begin to surface, some men shake and others cry. It is a very sad moment. They know they have done something wrong, and now they have been caught. They usually ask what will happen to them next. I tell them I need to report these findings to my superiors and they should think about contacting an attorney.

Reality can be painful, and these people often face jail or prison. Once evidence of a crime has been identified and turned over to my superiors, there is no turning back. Their lives are changed forever.

From Investigation to Conviction

For those who are investigated and subsequently arrested for the possession of child pornography, the process of protecting their legal rights is expensive, time-consuming, and socially embarrassing. There are several steps involved in the legal process.

Investigation: When state and/or federal authorities have reason to believe someone may have broken the law regarding child pornography, they can launch an investigation of the individual. The individual becomes a suspect in the commission of a crime.

The authorities may request an examination of the individual's home computer or obtain a warrant for an arrest or a search. Many times, authorities want to talk to the individual without an attorney present in the hopes of finding evidence and getting a confession. A confession is given verbally, but may also be written and signed by the suspect. This makes the case much stronger and easier to prosecute. Once a confession is given, the individual loses leverage in his ability to negotiate a favorable legal resolution.

Legal Counsel: An attorney who is hired by the suspect requires money in exchange for legal representation. This is called a "retainer." Suspects who cannot afford legal representation may be assigned a court-appointed attorney. Legal representation can be very expensive, and can run into the thousands of dollars. The cost can vary depending on the complexity of the case and the attorney's time commitment. It can also vary depending on whether the case is prosecuted by the state or federal authorities. Legal fees are much higher in federal prosecutions because of the greater complexity of federal law. Most suspects are shocked by the costs, and there is no guarantee that spending thousands of dollars can alter the outcome of the suspect's legal fate.

Arrest: A suspect who is arrested becomes a defendant in a legal case against him. The arrest can take place at home or even at work. This includes the possibility of being handcuffed in front of one's children or coworkers and being escorted to a police car for all to see. This step can be very intimidating and traumatic for all who witness the arrest.

The defendant is typically sent to jail and placed in a holding cell with other defendants. Fingerprints and pictures are taken by the police. The individual is placed in a holding cell until he or she goes to court for an arraignment. The charges are read in front of a judge, and the judge determines whether the defendant will be released from jail on bond. This requires a sum of money determined by the judge. The defendant remains out of jail until final sentencing, or until some condition of the bond is broken; for example, looking at child pornography.

Many months can elapse from the beginning of an investigation to prosecution and finally sentencing. The process includes additional court hearings, meeting with attorneys and the probation department, and most likely a referral for a psychological evaluation and/or counseling, sometimes referred to as a "sexual deviancy" evaluation.

Evaluations: Psychological/sexual deviancy evaluations can be requested by the defendant's attorney or ordered by the authority of the court. These evaluations are conducted by professionals who have credentials and expertise in this area. A typical evaluation includes a series of clinical interviews and psychological testing.

The goal of such interviews is to

• learn as much as possible about why the defendant was involved with child pornography.

• assess whether the defendant exhibits genuine remorse.

• assess relapse potential.

• assess amenability to treatment and determine which kind will be most beneficial.

• determine whether the defendant is a pedophile or sexual predator.

• address any question the attorney or court poses in the referral question, such as whether the defendant exhibits any signs of mental illness.

The goal of psychological testing is to collect additional data or information about the defendant. This can include assessment of the defendant's intellectual functioning, emotional and personality attributes, sexual deviancy attitudes, psychological and physical arousal patterns to children, and in general, the defendant's overall mental health.

This step also takes time and money to complete. The evaluator collects all the information and writes a report on the defendant. The report can be used by the court in determining the defendant's sentence.

Until an individual decides to plead guilty or is convicted after trial, care must be taken to protect the information shared between the psychological professional and the individual being evaluated. This confidentiality can be assured through one or more privileges, for example, lawyer/client privilege or doctor/patient privilege. However, since the law varies from jurisdiction to jurisdiction, it is important to address the confidentiality issue at the onset of the evaluation process.

Counseling: The defendant is referred to counseling by his attorney or by the court as a part of his sentencing. Counseling may include individual counseling or group counseling with others who have some type of sexual deviancy problem. The goal of counseling is to try to understand, in as much detail as possible, why the defendant committed the crime. This means talking about and understanding events that affected the defendant's curiosity, desire, and/or addiction to use pornography, and specifically child pornography. Counseling can take a year or more in most cases. It also costs money, and the court often wants to know how the defendant is progressing in counseling. The counselor may have to write a letter to update the probation department each month.

Sentencing: Finally, after many months and much anxiety and expense, the day of sentencing arrives. The defendant stands in front of the judge with his or her attorney. The courtroom is likely to be filled with other defendants await-ing their sentences, along with family members and other interested parties. The judge makes the final decision or judgment about the defendant's legal fate. Prison, jail, fines, probation, community service, loss of computer privileges, and inclusion on the state sex offender registry are all possible legal consequences. Loss of family, loss of job, and notoriety in the newspaper can change the way the defendant is viewed and treated by the community for the rest of his or her life.

Sentencing is a sobering moment in the lives of many offenders. Defendants often have no real idea as to the seriousness of their crime in the eyes of the community and court, but if a law is broken, the court must respond accordingly. Hearing the judge proclaim, "Mr. Smith, you are hereby sentenced to the Jackson Correctional Facility for a period of three to five years" is a powerful dose of reality.

Criminal Penalties

The potential legal consequences or penalties associated with child pornography may differ, depending on the state where the crime is committed. Regardless, the consequences are real and life changing.

As we've already mentioned, both Michigan and the federal government use sentencing guidelines to compute a sentencing range. A defendant can be charged at both the state and federal level. There are many factors that can influence the penalty, including physical and/or psychological injury to the victim, number of victims, criminal sexual penetration, and the defendant's criminal history. Under federal guidelines, a very long prison sentence (more than twenty years) is possible.

Michigan law has the following statutory maximum penalties:

Tier 1: not more than twenty years
Tier 2: not more than seven years
Tier 3: not more than four years

Tier 1 and computers: not more than twenty years
Tier 2 and computers: not more than ten years
Tier 3 and computers: not more than seven years

In federal law, the defendant is not eligible for parole and will likely serve the sentence imposed, less an allowance for good time, presently 15 percent of a person's sentence. Good time is not automatic. It must be earned by good behavior.

In Michigan law, a minimum and a maximum sentence is imposed. The maximum sentence is set by statute. The minimum sentence is set by the court. The minimum sentence is a parole eligibility date. However, eligibility is not the same as entitlement, and many Michigan prisoners serve well beyond their minimum dates.

Scriptural Guidance for Keeping Your Balance

There is a clear distinction between legal pornography and child pornography, which has profound legal consequences. Unfortunately, many people fail to notice when they are getting dangerously close to the edge of legality. It is as if they are dancing on the edge of a cliff. If they do not exercise control and restraint, they risk plummeting into the valley of serious legal and personal consequences.

The following episode of the life of the prophet Ezekiel can is a source of inspiration and tremendous hope for those living "on the edge."

> The hand of the LORD was on me, and he brought me out by the Spirit of the LORD and set me in the middle of a valley; it was full of bones. He led me back and forth among them, and I saw a great many bones on the floor of the valley, bones that were very dry. He asked me, "Son of man, can these bones live?"
>
> I said, "Sovereign LORD, you alone know."
>
> Then he said to me, "Prophesy to these bones and say to them, 'Dry bones, hear the word of the LORD! This is what the Sovereign LORD says to these bones: I will make breath enter you, and you will come to life. I will attach tendons to you and make flesh come upon you and cover you with skin; I will put breath in you, and you will come to life. Then you will know that I am the LORD.'"

So I prophesied as I was commanded. And as I was prophesying, there was a noise, a rattling sound, and the bones came together, bone to bone. I looked, and tendons and flesh appeared on them and skin covered them, but there was no breath in them.

Then he said to me, "Prophesy to the breath; prophesy, son of man, and say to it, 'This is what the Sovereign LORD says: Come, breath, from the four winds and breathe into these slain, that they may live.'" So I prophesied as he commanded me, and breath entered them; they came to life and stood up on their feet—a vast army.

Then he said to me: "Son of man, these bones are the whole house of Israel. They say, 'Our bones are dried up and our hope is gone; we are cut off.' Therefore prophesy and say to them: 'This is what the Sovereign LORD says: My people, I am going to open your graves and bring you up from them; I will bring you back to the land of Israel. Then you, my people, will know that I am the LORD, when I open your graves and bring you up from them. I will put my Spirit in you and you will live, and I will settle you in your own land. Then you will know that I the LORD have spoken, and I have done it, declares the LORD.'"

—Ezekiel 37:1-14

The context for this text from the prophecy of Ezekiel is the Babylonian captivity. In this seemingly hopeless situation, the Israelites lamented, "Our bones are dried up and our hope is gone." But God ordered the prophet Ezekiel to prophesy to the bones and tell them they would live again. God promised, "I am going to open your graves and bring you up from them; I will bring you back to the land of Israel."

God's message of hope and renewal was given through the prophet Ezekiel to the ancient Israelites held captive in

Babylon. But that message is also for all those who have been held captive by a life of cybersex and pornography. It is for all those who look around and see only decay, for those who believe, like the Israelites, that their situation is hopeless.

Prior to the Babylonian captivity, Israel had been stubborn and disobedient. They had bowed down and worshiped other gods. As punishment, God allowed Israel to be taken captive to Babylon, which became a "graveyard" for the people. At times their conditions were bearable, but most often they were oppressed. They couldn't build their life in this foreign land, and they couldn't go home. After twenty years of captivity, the Israelites began to lose hope. They started asking fundamental questions—questions like, *Where is God? Why hasn't God delivered us? Why is this happening to us?*

According to Psalm 137, the people were so distraught that they couldn't even sing their beloved songs of faith. They hung up their harps and sat, bitter and despondent, by the banks of the river Chebar. They were unable to experience God's presence. They felt spiritually dead, alone, abandoned.

Perhaps, like the ancient Israelites, you feel spiritually dead. Perhaps you wonder if you can even consider yourself a Christian anymore. Perhaps you are unable to pray, unable to sing, unable to hope.

Your spouse also knows what it's like to feel abandoned and rejected. His or her life has been shattered by your Internet infidelity. The promises you made to your partner have been broken as you have been held captive by the dark forces of pornography. Your spouse laments that your marriage may never be as enjoyable and meaningful as it once was.

This story from Ezekiel reminds us that God had compassion on his exiled people. Since the time of their father Abraham, God had promised the Israelites a land, a home that would define them as a nation. God gave the exiles hope that they would return to occupy their land, rebuild their lives, restore their homes, and start anew. God promised to raise their dead spirits from their graves. He commanded Ezekiel to tell the people, "I will put my Spirit in you, and you will live, and I will settle you in your own land."

The phrase "I will put my Spirit in you" is important because it speaks of promise, of rebirth, of new life, of hope. In the original Hebrew language, the word "Spirit," or *ru'ah* may also be translated as "wind" or "breath." This word is a word of life—the creative, life-giving force of God. It is found in many of the stories of Scripture:

> In the beginning God created the heavens and the earth. Now the earth was formless and empty, darkness was over the surface of the deep, and the Spirit *[ru'ah]* of God was hovering over the waters.
>
> —Genesis 1:1-2

> Then the Lord God formed a man from the dust of the ground and breathed into his nostrils the breath *[ru'ah]* of life, and the man became a living being.
>
> —Genesis 2:7

> But God remembered Noah and all the wild animals and the livestock that were with him in the ark, and he sent a wind *[ru'ah]* over the earth, and the waters receded.
>
> —Genesis 8:1

These stories are of creation. Creation out of chaos. Creation with a purpose. Creation given form and life by God alone. And once again, in the passage from Ezekiel, the Israelites hear the words of creation: "I will put my Spirit *[ru'ah]* in you and you will live."

God's promise of renewed life that Ezekiel proclaimed to the Israelites is still available to you this very day. Like the Israelites in the graveyard called Babylon, you may sometimes feel dead although you are alive. But God has not abandoned you. Ezekiel's vision is a powerful demonstration of God's creative and sustaining love that breathes life back into even the driest of bones.

Strategies for Reestablishing Order

It's important to understand the legal risks associated with child pornography. The best way to avoid legal problems associated with child pornography is to resist looking at, collecting, trading, or saving pictures or movies to your computer's hard drive or discs. If there are no pictures, there is no crime, no fear of investigation and prosecution. Life is more peaceful when you live within the law.

The following are two intervention strategies that can be used to curb the desire for and use of child pornography: reality therapy and aversive imagery

Reality Therapy

This strategy encourages those who are tempted by the desire to look at child pornography to immediately focus on the legal consequences: jail or prison. The fear of legal consequences can counter any pleasure associated with looking at pornography, because thinking about going to prison is very unpleasant. Such feelings can stop sexual arousal dead in its tracks. So the reality of going to prison can act as a deterrent to using pornography.

Some common consequences associated with using child pornography include the following:

- Shame and loss of dignity
- Living in fear of legal consequences
- Divorce, loss of family and children

- Legal expense related to criminal defense running into thousands of dollars
- Getting fired from your job
- Being identified in the newspaper or television after arrest
- Being placed on the sex offender registry
- Psychological stress (depression, anxiety, fear)
- Jail, prison, probation

Aversive Imagery

This is another technique used to reduce or eliminate undesirable thoughts, fantasies, behaviors, or feelings associated with using child pornography. It involves pairing unwanted thoughts with some type of aversive, or unpleasant, image. Here's how it works:

Step 1: Identify thoughts, feelings, fantasies, or behaviors that need to be changed. Make a list of them. Common examples include the following:

- I want to look at child pornography right now.

- I turn on the computer and right away start surfing pornography websites. It's only a matter of time before I start looking for pictures of children.

- When I'm at work, I picture myself going home and using the computer for pornography after my spouse goes to bed.

- I'm on my favorite sports website, and suddenly, my mind drifts to thinking about porn sites.

- I'm sexually frustrated and begin to think of child pictures for excitement and release.

- I'm thinking about children and I can't get rid of the thoughts.

- I was watching television when my wife said she had to go to the store. As soon as she left, I went upstairs and started surfing pornography.

Step 2: Identify, stop, and replace these thoughts and feelings with an aversive image. Imagine something very unpleasant. The more graphic and disturbing the image, the better it will work. The goal is to immediately eliminate a thought or feeling that is sexually arousing by replacing it with an image that stops the arousal. For example, imagine being arrested at home in front of your wife and children. The police handcuff you and escort you to the police car. As you're driven away, you look up and see your children waving goodbye and crying in the front window.

This aversive image is reality based: it can and does happen to people. Those who have gone through the experience of seeing their children crying and waving goodbye as they are taken away by the authorities never forget it. It is imprinted on their memory forever. An image like this can be an effective way to stop the sexual arousal associated with child pornography. Keep in mind that you will need to discover an image that is effective for you. This process may take time.

Step 3: Practice, practice, and practice some more. For this technique to be effective, you'll need to practice it over time. Eventually the aversive image will be automatic and will become an effective way to reduce sexual arousal associated with child pornography.

Using both techniques described above—the fear of legal consequences and aversive imagery—can be an effective way to combat the desire for using child pornography.

Questions for Reflection and Discussion

1. What is child pornography? Why is it so important to understand the definition?

2. "Most people who look at child pornography should not be confused with sexual predators or pedophiles." Do you agree that this is a valid distinction? Why or why not?

3. How does looking at child pornography reinforce worldwide child abuse?

4. Criminal prosecution and jail time are very real possibilities for those who view child pornography. How effective are these consequences at deterring people from becoming involved with child pornography? How can "getting caught" help someone who is addicted to child pornography change his or her life?

Chapter 9

The Innocent Lambs

Protecting Our Children

Amy's Story

"Mom, come here—hurry! Look at this!"

I jumped out of my seat, peered over Amy's shoulder, and read what someone was typing to her in an instant message. I could not believe my eyes. There, in graphic detail, were proclamations of what this person wanted to do sexually with my daughter. He even wanted to send her a picture of himself naked! I told Amy to shut off the computer immediately. Later that night, we had a long talk.

* * *

Amy was thirteen when she first started using the Internet. She is our oldest child, so the cyberspace thing was new to us. Like many parents, we bought a computer and connected to the Internet because we thought it would benefit our family, especially our kids. We didn't want them to feel "different" from their friends or have them fall behind in their studies. Amy's teachers encouraged the use of the computer to help with homework. In fact, kids were required to take computer lab at school. So buying one for our home seemed like the natural thing to do.

Amy began using the Internet right away. She often "talked" online with her friends after school. Sometimes it seemed like she was on the computer all night.

Once in a while, Amy actually used the computer for homework. She could always find what she needed online when researching a topic for a paper or project. It was easier, not to mention quicker, than going to the library like we used to do.

As her time online grew, so did our struggles over the computer. Her dad and I began setting limits on her usage. Of course, she accused us of "ruining" her social life because of these restrictions.

The night that Amy and I had our long talk, she told me she had seen dirty pictures on the Internet. I was shocked, but calmly asked to know more. She told me they just "popped up" while she was working on a school project. She knew she shouldn't look at them and tried closing out the website, but more pictures kept popping up. She had to turn off the computer to make them go away and then restart it. She also told me she'd received e-mail from strangers, and sometimes they contained sexual themes. She had no idea how any of them got her e-mail address.

Amy promised me she had never gone to a pornography site on her own or responded to any of those e-mails. I was relieved when she told me that. Amy's always been a responsible child and we had no reason not to trust her.

We went into the "history" of received e-mails on the computer. Amy was right. She had received an e-mail from an unknown source. It was entitled "Haven't talked lately." Amy had opened it, thinking it was sent by a friend she hadn't talked to in a long time. When we opened it together that night, it immediately linked us to a porn site. Graphic pictures of adults engaging in sex appeared. I was so angry! Who would send such a despicable thing to a child? I didn't want Amy to be exposed to this trash. I decided it was time to educate myself more about the dangers of the Internet. Here is some of what I have since discovered:

The Internet is a pornography minefield. Never in my wildest dreams did I imagine the multitudes of pornographic pictures, movies, and websites available on the Internet. In fact, if your child is doing research and types in a keyword or phrase to search online, it's very possible that the list of sites that shows up will include some links to pornography sites. For example, say your child is doing research on the government and wants information on the White House. One of the sites including the words "white house" in its domain name was actually a porn site! Pornographers often purchase innocent-sounding or popular domain names to purposefully mislead people to their sites.

Anticipate uninvited guests. You may not realize how easy it is for strangers to talk to children online. Some Internet service providers (ISPs) offer a membership directory that allows all subscribers to that ISP to search for other subscribers. Most people, like my Amy, make up a member profile that describes who they are, their interests, or any other personal information they care to share. Most kids think this is a fun—and harmless—way to communicate with others. However, profiles make it easy for anyone to find your screen name in the directory, read up on your interests, and then send you an instant message.

You've probably read in the newspaper or heard on TV about situations where predators use the Internet to contact children. It really does happen, and their intentions are anything but innocent. Some will talk in a very sexual manner to kids. Others will try to win over a child's trust, build up her confidence, and then form an online "relationship."

One mother told me of a situation where her daughter was being stalked online. Every time she signed on, some guy sent her messages, wanting to chat. He'd tell her how sexy and pretty she was and try to get her to chat on the phone. He even sent her a picture of himself. Thank goodness she reported this to her mother and they blocked the guy from being able to contact her. But many children do not tell their parents, and secret relationships do develop. As a parent, we need to be aware of potential dangers so we can protect our children.

Beware of chatrooms. Like websites, there are some good ones and some that are not so good. They allow people with similar interests to meet in a "room" and "talk." (What you see is a real-time dialogue on the screen.) Chatrooms are set up by theme: friends, sports, dating, and so forth. Many rooms, however, have themes that are sexual in nature, and people of all ages—children included—can access these rooms. You need to be aware that even "innocent" chatrooms with teen themes are prime targets for pedophiles or predators who are looking for children. Such criminals spend a lot of time thinking of ways to gain access to children. The Internet practically delivers them to their door.

I do not want my daughter or any child exposed to or threatened by these people. That's why I've gone to such great lengths to educate my family on the dangers of the Internet. Please do the same for yourself and your children—before it's too late.

The Internet: A Pedophile's Playground

The Internet can be a dangerous place for our children. The abundance and availability of pornography is mind-boggling. Sexual predators have access to a virtual playground of children. Instead of going to the mall and parks, they can simply cruise the Internet looking for vulnerable children to exploit.

Richard B. Maring, chief executive officer of the Tribinium Corporation, has devoted himself to protecting children from the dangers of online pornography and predators. His website provides information and resources to combat this international problem. The following statistics are taken from www.innocenceonline.com:[1]

- The average age of boys when they are first exposed to pornography on the Internet is eight-and-a-half. For girls, it's eleven.

- According to Family Safe Media, 90 percent of children between the ages of eight and sixteen have viewed online pornography, most while doing homework.

- At least twenty-six children's characters, including Pokemon and Action Man, have been linked to thousands of porn sites.

- Twenty-one percent of teens say they have looked at something on the Internet that they wouldn't want their parents to know about.

- One in five children ages ten to seventeen have received a sexual solicitation over the Internet.

- Three million of the visitors to adult websites in September 2000 were under the age of eighteen.

- One in four children who use the Internet are exposed to unwanted sexual material.

- One in seventeen children ages ten to seventeen was threatened or harassed over the Internet in 2000.

- Seventy percent of sexual advances over the Internet happened while youths were on a home computer.

- A survey of 600 households conducted by the National Center of Missing and Exploited Children found that 20 percent of parents do not know any of their children's Internet passwords, instant messaging nicknames, or e-mail addresses.

- Only 5 percent of parents recognized the acronym POS (parent over shoulder) and only 1 percent could identify WTGP (want to go private?), both of which are used frequently by teens when instant messaging.

- Incidents of child sexual exploitation have risen from 4,573 cases in 1998 to 112,083 cases in 2004, according to the National Center for Missing and Exploited Children.

- Ninety-six percent of kids have gone online. Seventy-four percent have access at home and 61 percent use the Internet on a typical day.

- Twenty percent of youths have received sexual solicitations online. Eighty-nine percent of sexual solicitations were made in chatrooms.

Scriptural Guidance for Training Children in Faith

Hear, O Israel: The LORD our God, the LORD is one. Love the LORD your God with all your heart and with all your soul and with all your strength. These commandments that I give you today are to be on your hearts. Impress them on your children. Talk about them when you sit at home and when you walk along the road, when you lie down and when you get up. Tie them as symbols on your hands and bind them on your foreheads. Write them on the doorframes of your houses and on your gates.

—Deuteronomy 6:4-9

Near the end of four decades of wandering in the desert, the Israelites heard Moses describe what life would be like in the promised land. They knew they would be confronted with and influenced by people whose values, lifestyles, and beliefs were altogether different from their own. It was essential for them to devise a strategy for surviving as the people of God. And so Moses spoke to the Israelites saying, "Hear, O Israel: the LORD our God, the LORD is one. Love the LORD your God with all your heart and with all your soul and with all your strength."

This passage from Deuteronomy is called the Shema. It comprises the most important scriptural command of the Jewish faith. Faithful Jews repeat the Shema twice a day, and many have it inscribed on the entryway into their homes, reminding them of their faith every time they enter the house.

During his ministry, Jesus referred to this passage as the most important commandment in the entire Bible. Thus this text from Deuteronomy serves as the very foundation of what Christians need to teach their children in order for them to grow a strong faith.

What does it mean to "love the LORD your God with all your heart and with all your soul and with all your strength"?

"Heart" refers to spirit, that part of you that is able to worship and have a relationship with God. "Soul" includes the rest of your personality—mind, emotions, and will. "Strength" refers to your physical body. So this verse means that our love for God must consume every part of our being—body, soul, and spirit.

Ever since Moses first spoke those words, people wanting their children to have a vibrant faith in God have followed this command. But Christians who live in the twenty-first century face a particularly difficult challenge because we live within a culture where human relationships and sexuality are debased through pornography. Nonetheless, Moses' words still provide helpful guidance for parents who want their children to grow in the faith.

The first principle to be learned from this passage is being an example. In verse 6, Moses says, "These commandments that I give you today are to be upon your hearts." In other words, parents are to model or demonstrate through their own behavior what faithfulness means. This is exceptionally important because children are very impressionable. Children watch their parents and in most cases pattern their own behavior after what they observe. Moreover, children are extremely perceptive and quickly recognize whether the faith their parents profess fits with the way their parents live. In addition, children often mimic what they observe in the culture around them. Children want to be seen, especially by their peers, as "cool," "normal," and "acceptable." That is why the Internet poses such a danger. It includes a vast cultural smorgasbord, but much of it does not meet the standards Christian parents want to instill in their children.

As a parent, your best defense in the battle for your kids' souls is your example. By your example, have your children learned what it means for a husband and wife to express mutual respect? Have they learned about marital loyalty and devotion? Have they learned to express affection appropriately? Have they learned that sexuality is to be celebrated within the context of a covenant relationship?

In verse 7, Moses says we need to "impress [the commandments] on your children." Both the Revised Standard Version and the King James Version translate the Hebrew as "teach diligently," while Today's New International Version translates it as "impress." The literal meaning of the Hebrew is "to say something twice" or "to repeat." The word originally referred to the sharpening of a blade or a tool by rubbing it repeatedly against the whetstone. Over time, the meaning of the word evolved, first from the act of sharpening, then to a piercing action, and finally to the process of teaching. The basic idea behind this verse, then, is that by repeating the teachings of the faith, parents will eventually infuse these beliefs into the hearts and minds of their children.

"Talk about them when you sit at home and when you walk along the road, when you lie down and when you get up." That is to say, teach your children in every situation in life—morning, noon, and night. When you are at home, teach them. When you are driving to the grocery store, teach them. When you are on vacation, teach them. When you help them say their prayers, teach them.

Teach your children that God is the Creator. Show them the beauty and intricacies of nature and teach them that it is all by God's design. Teach them about sin, about the difference between right and wrong, and about how our behavior can distance us from God and from each other. Teach them about Jesus and how his redemptive love reconciles us to God. Teach them about the active, living Spirit of God that guides and comforts us along life's journey. Teach them about sexual morality and sexual self-control, and encourage them to celebrate their sexuality as a God-given gift to be treated honorably. Teach them that death is a part of life, but because of the grace of God we can look forward to eternal life in a renewed creation. Talk to them about things such as these when you are sitting at home, or out for a walk, when you go to sleep at night, and when you rise in the morning!

It's up to you to teach your children to live devoted and faithful lives as followers of Jesus Christ.

Shielding the Innocence of Children

Amy's experience is similar to that of many young people who use the Internet for fun and communication with their friends. It's become a popular way to socialize. Like Amy, many kids are unaware of the potential dangers online.

At any given moment, there are thousands of sexual predators who want to chat with children. They work hard to engage kids in conversation, searching for weaknesses while trying to build rapport. Their goal is to gain enough personal information to allow them to proceed to the next level: engaging in sexual chat online or over the phone or meeting in person to engage in sexual activity.

Predators hide in the darkness of cyberspace. Don't be fooled into thinking that just because you can't see them, they're not out there. They want kids to believe they've found a trusted friend who understands them better than their parents do. They've often had extensive experience talking with children, and the anonymity of the Internet emboldens them and reinforces their fantasies.

They prowl around on the Internet in places kids frequent, looking to make a connection with a child. They know it's only a matter of time before they'll succeed. If they're lucky, they'll even convince someone to meet them offline. What happens next often makes the news, and the details can be frightening.

Predators have always known where kids congregate, and the Internet has opened up a new "playground" for them to frequent. Often they pass themselves off as teenagers and young adults. Some go for a more "honest" approach, admitting they are adults and acting as a supportive parental figure to win over a child's trust. Never underestimate the ability of predators to gain access to kids. They spend a lot of time analyzing and developing different approaches.

Parents need to understand and accept that although the Internet can be a very dangerous place, they are not helpless to protect their children. They can educate themselves, establish family rules for using the Internet, and talk with their kids about the very real dangers lurking in cyberspace.

As a parent, you may have to overcome your own fears in order to broach this subject with your children. A conversation about the dangers of the Internet with kids—especially if they're teens—can be difficult. They may believe and act like they know everything. But they don't have the life experience you do, and they still need you, despite their push for independence. Tell them that your reason for the discussion is because you love them and want to protect them. They may still tune you out or argue about the rules you implement. But in time they will realize that you've backed up your verbal declarations of love with actions.

Remember that if you don't educate your kids, there are many on the Internet who are willing to do it for you. That thought should send any fears you may have packing.

Safety Tips for Kids

Please review these basic safeguards with your children.

- Never give out personal information about yourself or your family (name, address, phone number, e-mail address, or passwords).
- Never give a stranger a photo of yourself. Let your friends know not to pass out your pictures either. Once a photo is sent out over the Internet, you can never get it back. It can be traded and passed on to others hundreds of times. A picture identifies who you are. Some predators, having gotten hold of pictures and general locations of children, look for them—sometimes successfully.
- Never meet people you've met through the Internet offline. Never! You may think you know them, but you have no idea whether they really are who they say they are. People lie about age, sex, and other personal factors all the time.
- Never accept e-mails, pictures, or instant messages from strangers.
- Tell a parent if someone online tries to engage you in sexual chat. Cyber-crime can and should be reported to the police.
- If a friend is threatened or harassed online or tells you she plans on meeting someone offline, tell your parents and hers immediately. Your friend may be upset with you, but that phone call may save her life.

On Blogs and Bullying

A blog is like a personal diary, but it allows others to read what you post (unless it is password-protected). Some people write about their interests, while others keep a daily or weekly journal. Blogs often include pictures, and they may also include an invitation for the public (or those invited to view your blog) to comment on what you've posted. Two sites that are extremely popular with teens, Facebook and MySpace, offer online services allowing people to set up their own blogs.

Sometimes teens use blogs, as well as e-mail and instant messages, to anonymously pick on, intimidate, or threaten their peers. This is called "cyberbullying," and it can cause great emotional distress. Moreover, it's difficult to stop a bully you can't identify.

Cyberbullies have discovered a new way to use the Internet for sexual exploitation called "cyberblackmail." For example, a teenage boy may threaten a girl who goes to his school by saying he will spread bad rumors about her at school unless she takes her clothes off and performs sexual acts in front of a video recorder attached to a computer. The "show" is telecast over the Internet, and the boy watches it on his home computer. Even if he promises to keep it private, he is likely to forward the images to other boys to watch on their computers. Often the girl has no clue about how many of her peers have watched her on the Internet until the information is passed around school. She is exploited and humiliated.

Filtering and Accountability Software

As the proliferation of pornography on the Internet continues to escalate, so does the need to protect children from exposure to harmful images. A number of products that block pornographic visual content and graphic language are currently on the market, and new technologies continue to emerge. Some of the more popular products include the following:

- Bsecure
- CyberPatrol
- CyberSentinel
- CYBERsitter
- FilterPak
- McAfee Parental Controls
- Net Nanny
- Norton Parental Controls
- Safe Eyes
- SeeNoEvil
- WiseChoice.net

In addition to filtering or cloaking software, software is available that can be used to keep people accountable, such as Covenant Eyes or X3watch. These products monitor Internet use and e-mail reports to a designated accountability partner. Some actually keep a record of every key stroke (therefore keeping track of the content of e-mails and Instant Messages) while others track search engine requests and web pages that have been viewed. Some companies that make accountability software bundle their product with filtering software.

In Amy's Words

When my mom started talking to me about how I needed to make some changes in how I use the Internet, I threw a fit. It wasn't fair that I had to change my screen name and online profile just because some creep tried to talk dirty to me!

However, once I started really listening to what my mom had to say, I began to see things from her point of view. I never realized that people I didn't know—and didn't want to know—could learn so much about me through the Internet. I mean, it's scary when you really think about it.

My mom also doesn't want me going into any chatrooms. I'd heard about them from my friends and I didn't think anything was wrong with them. But my mom says that men go into these rooms, sometimes pretending to be teenagers—even girl teenagers! Gross! Some get off just by talking to you, but others are sexual predators who try to befriend you and get you to meet them. Now I know why she doesn't want my personal contact information getting out there.

I know you're not supposed to give out your name, phone number, or address to anyone you don't know, but some of these guys online are really persistent. They'll keep instant messaging you anytime they see you're online. I now know how to block these creeps, and I've changed my screen name and profile too. It no longer contains any identifying information.

It was a bit of a hassle to make these changes, and I'm still ticked that there are so many weirdos in the world who make it necessary. But I know my mom really loves me since she took the time to learn about this stuff and even put up with me yelling at her when she first started talking about it.

Some of my friends don't understand why my parents are so strict about the Internet. I just tell them what my mom and dad always tell me: It's better to be safe than sorry.

A Word from a Sexual Predator

I surf the Internet hunting for girls. I prefer them between the ages of twelve and fifteen. There's something about this age range that drives me crazy. The girls are so cute and innocent.

Many men have the same fantasy. We go to parks, playgrounds, and the mall. We go where the girls go. Sometimes we just watch them. Sometimes we follow them. And sometimes we even strike up a conversation with them.

Some men prefer boys, but girls are my desire. I've taken pictures of them with my digital camera without them suspecting a thing. I make up sexual fantasies about the girls in the pictures and masturbate to them.

Now the Internet has brought many of these girls to my doorstep. It's made my pursuit much easier. There are so many naive girls online—and their parents are even worse. They think that just because their child is on the home computer, she's somehow safe from guys like me.

When I make contact with her with my screen name, DaddyTeddyBear, she won't suspect a thing. I have more than one screen name, but I use this one most often. All my screen names project warmth and kindness. It's important to make the girls feel safe with me.

My profile makes me sound like a really nice guy. I describe how I like animals, sunsets, and buying things for girls. Girls like it when you buy them things.

I find most of my conquests by surfing chatrooms teen girls like to frequent. I read their profiles and then try to establish contact with them in the chatroom or through an instant message. I always start out by asking how her day is going. Then I'll make a positive comment about something in her profile.

Once she's talking to me I start the "grooming" process. This is how I get her to trust me. I ask about school, her boyfriend, her parents. I look for any indication that she's lonely or having problems with her parents. Girls will tell you so much about themselves when they're upset or feeling needy. I give them a shoulder to cry on and convince them that I'm their ally.

If I feel it's safe to ask them questions about their physical appearance, I'll take the risk. I'll say how pretty she must be, or how the boys must be all over her. Then I'll ask her if she's alone. If she is, I'll steer the conversation toward sex. I usually start by asking if her boyfriend is a good kisser. If she responds positively, then I know there's a good chance she'll discuss sexual experiences in greater detail. Hearing about real-life sexual experiences is very arousing. Often I'll masturbate while she talks.

In time, as I gain her trust, I'll ask her to send me a picture of herself. I'll ask if she wants to see me naked. Some girls say yes. Some have sent naked pictures of themselves in return.

My ultimate goal is to meet these girls offline. I tell them I'll buy them something if we meet. I won't pressure them for sex, but in my fantasy they'll want to have sex after we meet. I make them promise never to tell anyone about our conversations. I tell them adults, especially parents, won't understand. I tell them how much I value their friendship and want it to continue. I tell them they are special, and I want to take care of them. If we meet, we meet in a public place. If they get scared or back out at this point, I simply go back to a chatroom and start all over again.

So I'm curious—do you know who your children talk to online? Can you be sure? I'll promise you this: If you aren't watching over your children, somebody else is. It may be someone like me.

Questions for Reflection and Discussion

1. How has the Internet become a dangerous place for children? What are the benefits of the Internet for kids?

2. What steps can parents, teachers, and youth pastors take to keep children safe from sexual predators on the Internet?

3. What, if anything, did you find surprising about the statistics on pages 199-200 about the scope of the problem of predators on the web?

4. If you are a parent, how much do you know about your children's Internet usage?

Chapter 10

Creating Order Out of Chaos

Recovery from Cybersexual Addiction

Larry's Story

It was my turn to speak. All eyes were fixed on me. Heart pounding, I took a deep breath, rose from my seat and spoke the words all were waiting to hear, "Hello, I'm Larry, and I'm a sex addict." The group members broke into loud applause and a roar of approval.

I recently discovered I have a sexual addiction problem. I go to counseling and attend a twelve-step recovery program called Sexual Addiction Anonymous. It's a support group for men and women who struggle with sexual addiction, very similar to Alcoholics Anonymous. People talk about their problems and support each other. No one criticizes or judges harshly. I feel safe there.

I never realized that sex could become addictive. I thought all guys liked sex as much as I did. I also never realized that many good men, particularly men of faith, shared a similar struggle. This was a surprising revelation to me. But it was also comforting to know I was not alone in my struggles.

My journey of discovering I was a sex addict has been a painful one, but there's also a sense of freedom in admitting I have a problem.

My counselor and my wife have reassured me that it takes a lot of courage to admit to one's problems. For years, I struggled in silence, keeping my secret all to myself. I was afraid to look at myself in the mirror and admit I had a weakness. Maybe it was pride, or the fear that others would look down on me if they knew my secret. I tried hard to be a good man of faith, but I often felt like a failure. It was like living a double life.

I cared about God and my family, but I could not handle the thought of my wife and children finding out my secret. My children looked up to me. They put me on a pedestal. My wife trusted me, and I've always tried to set a good Christian example. Deep inside, I knew I was betraying God and my faith. Despite my prayers asking God to help me stop, lust and sex seemed to control me. I knew what I was doing was wrong, but there were times I didn't really want to stop. I had made so many promises to stop, and each time I broke them. I reached a point where I was so discouraged that I doubted whether I could really stop at all.

* * *

My story begins when I was a teenager—back in the 70s, before computers. I heard about sex and girls at school. The guys at school talked about finding *Playboy* magazines in their parents' bedroom, usually hidden in a closet or box. Like any curious boy, I searched my parents' bedroom like a detective on a mission. To my amazement and excitement, I found my first *Playboy* magazine and a book of short stories with sexual themes in my father's dresser. They were hidden under his T-shirts.

I felt I had hit the jackpot. I was thirteen, at that curious age, and I was overwhelmed by the excitement of seeing naked women. It was a real adrenaline rush. I looked over each page very carefully. I didn't want to miss a thing. The women were so attractive. They exposed their breasts in plain view, and they were big breasts too. I sensed I was doing something wrong that I could get in trouble for, but the risk was worth it. I put down the magazine and started to read through my father's book.

The book didn't have any pictures in it, but each chapter described some type of sexual scene. It was very graphic. I'd never read anything like it before, and I'd never read a book so fast. I thought I'd found something very special. When I finished, I put the material back very carefully just the way I found it. I didn't want to get caught. I knew I'd found something exciting, but I also sensed it might be wrong. I listened for the car to pull up in the driveway. All day long I thought about the pictures and stories. At bedtime I dreamed about the girls in the pictures. I couldn't wait until my parents left me alone again. When they did, I went back to the magazine and book. I memorized the pictures and stories.

We were a church family, and it seemed strange that my own father had pornography. I wondered if my mother knew about this. I was confused, but to this day, I never told my dad what I found. As time went on, I would go back to the drawer again. I used to wait for my parents to leave so I could hunt for more pornography. Every month, a new magazine would appear.

I was sexually excited by all the pictures and eventually started to masturbate. As my counselor told me, the good feelings I got from masturbating reinforced my early desires for pornography. Even though I felt guilty, I never told anyone, especially the guys at school. I didn't want to get in trouble, and I certainly didn't want them to know I was masturbating. I was afraid I'd be teased to death.

* * *

Throughout my teen years, I struggled with masturbation and the desire for pornography. I went back to my dad's drawer for years and never got caught. There were always new magazines to look at. I started to masturbate more and more. It was a craving that had to be satisfied. When I could not access the magazines, I'd just visualize the pictures in my head. The images were so powerful.

When I got older and went to college, I continued to struggle with pornography. I dismissed it as a problem because I told myself all guys looked at pornography and masturbated. I thought it was harmless and normal. I did not realize I was forming an addictive pattern to sex. Sexual addiction was not a concept that was talked about in college.

In school I dated but was somewhat socially insecure and shy. I lacked social confidence. Girls did not find me that attractive; I felt rejected by the most popular and good-looking girls. I wanted to date more, but relationships never seemed to last that long. And even when I was dating, my desire for pornography did not decrease.

* * *

My desire for pornography continued well after I married. I thought I'd have no need for pornography, and I stopped for a while. After a short period of time, my desire came back. I'd buy magazines and videos and hide them from my wife. I suggested we look at pornography together, but she had no interest and became angered at what she considered a very strange request. I told her I was just kidding. My wife had no clue how serious my interest in pornography was at the time. I made sure I had a good hiding place where she would never find it. I knew I'd be ashamed if she ever caught me.

There was a dirty bookstore about two miles from where we lived. I started to go there and watch X-rated movies in small booths. It was dirty and smelly, and the floors were sticky. There were holes in the walls where you could watch someone masturbate. Sometimes you'd see two guys coming out of the same booth. I knew what they were doing in there, but despite being grossed out, I went back to the bookstore. It was like being in a secret club. Guys would look at each other. We all knew why we were there. There was a feeling of acceptance. A few men made passes at me, but I resisted them. I always left feeling guilty and dirty. When I came home, I'd immediately take a shower and wash my clothes. I was trying to wash away the guilt.

* * *

Eventually we moved to a new city out of state. There were no dirty bookstores around, so that problem took care of itself. I was actually relieved.

One day, while renting a regular movie at the local video store, I noticed a door that said "adults only" on it. I peeked into the room and noticed that the walls were covered with X-rated videos. How could this be at a "family" video store?

I walked in and left with an "adult" movie. When I'd see mothers and their children in the store, I'd always pretend to be looking at regular movies, wait for them to check out first, and when the coast was clear, I'd dash to the counter and try to get out of there as soon as possible. It was embarrassing to check out a dirty movie from some young kid. Many times the clerk was a girl. I could never look her in the eye. I always paid cash, and I worried that someone might recognize me. What would I say? I felt guilty and sleazy and made many promises to stop. But each time I broke the promise and felt more ashamed.

* * *

My struggle with sexual addiction escalated when we bought a home computer and connected to the Internet. I stopped going to the video store altogether. I found all the pornography I wanted online. This was perfect. It was free and anonymous. I no longer had to face the clerk in the video store or risk being seen by someone I knew.

At first, I spent countless hours surfing the Internet for pornography. There are places called "galleries"—pornography sites where pictures are stored and collected. Many sites are organized by theme: amateur wives, teens, group sex, and the like. You simply click the theme you're interested in, and a picture appears on your computer screen. It's that easy and quick.

It's like going to a buffet. The pornographers even refer to it as a "menu." Pictures often appear as "thumbnails"—very small pictures. Click on the small picture, and within seconds it enlarges on the computer screen. With the speed of the Internet, hundreds of different websites and pictures can be viewed during the course of an hour. Many sites tempt you with free pictures because they want you to pay a monthly fee and become a member. A member gets "VIP" status. This means they get more pictures on a daily and monthly basis than nonmembers. There seemed to be an endless supply.

* * *

The Internet also allows you to view pornographic movies. The faster the computer, the clearer the movie appears. They look like movies you could buy or rent from a store, complete with "trailers"—free, thirty-second samples of full-length movies. If the sample hooks your interest and desire, you can buy the movie online and download it into the computer. You get instant gratification and avoid detection since pornographic movies do not arrive in the mail.

Some people buy webcams—small cameras that attach to the computer. They use the camera to take pictures of themselves and send them to someone who wants to look at them. These cameras are very easy to purchase at stores carrying computer equipment. They are very small and easy to hide when not in use.

* * *

As the initial excitement of Internet pornography began to wear off, I discovered chatrooms. These are set up by an online service or by members of the service. All are identified by themes. I was shocked to see rooms with themes about children and incest. I visited these rooms and watched the sexual conversations about children, but I never talked in those rooms. I found them disgusting. Instead, I started to explore several chatrooms that contained themes about wives. I watched and listened, and when I became comfortable, I began discussing my wife in the chatrooms. Many men traded pictures of their wives with others. I was asked many times to trade pictures of my wife as well. I downloaded pictures of women off the Internet and pretended they were my wife and traded them. It was like a trading club. Some wanted to engage in "private" conversations and discuss their fantasies, many of which included watching their wives in some type of sexual act with other men. This activity was called "trading" or "sharing."

I found a chatroom entitled "offline chat about wives." Curious, I visited the room and was instantly hooked. Men found other men to trade pictures and start a sexual conversation about a fantasy of their wives. This progressed to discussing the fantasy by phone. I tried "phone sex" with several men, but I never gave anyone my home or work phone number. Instead I bought a phone card at the local gas station and used this to call. There were many men willing to share their numbers, so it was easy to find someone to chat with. The conversations would turn sexual very quickly. Both parties engaged in masturbation at the same time. When one or both reached orgasm, the phone call usually ended abruptly. I felt ashamed and dirty after each call. Several times I promised to quit, but each time I broke the promise. At the pinnacle of my addiction, I was looking at pornography every day and had phone sex once a week.

* * *

One night when my wife had fallen asleep on the sofa downstairs, I went upstairs to surf the Internet for pornography and sexual chat. The house was quiet and the children were asleep. I thought it was safe to go online. In the middle of a sexual conversation with a man, I had a pornographic image of a woman enlarged on my computer screen. My wife walked into the bedroom and caught me masturbating. She was shocked and angry. We had a long talk that night as I broke down and told her of my struggles with pornography.

When she calmed down, she suggested I call our pastor the next day. I called him first thing in the morning and met him to discuss this issue. He recognized that I had a sexual addiction problem and referred me to a specialist who treats these problems. It was a very, very embarrassing meeting, but I disclosed the truth. I wound up going to counseling and a twelve-step support group for sexual addicts. It was a turning point in my life. I made a commitment to get this problem under control.

It has been a challenging road to recovery. Although there have been times when I have slipped up and looked at pornography again, I've worked hard to get the problem under control. My life was chaos, and I was drifting further into the dark side of sexual addiction. Thank goodness my pastor was willing to talk to me openly about my problem and help me get back on the right path.

The Chaos of Sexual Addiction

Larry is a sex addict. This means he has developed a psychological dependency on sex—in this case, Internet pornography. Larry's case is important to understand because it demonstrates how curiosity about pornography can escalate into an addictive pattern and become a destructive habit over time. Some people become addicted within weeks; others progress into addiction over months. Everyone's pattern is unique.

Larry was once an innocent little boy who knew nothing about sexuality and the dangers of pornography. The seeds of his addiction were unknowingly planted by his father, who hid pornography in his home. Imagine how Larry's life might have been different if his father had not used pornography.

Instead of keeping his youthful innocence, Larry began to crave pornography and the feelings of arousal and pleasure associated with it. Like an alcoholic who craves his drug, Larry craved pornography.

Larry was socially insecure as a child and teen, and pornography filled a void in his life. It made him feel good. It helped him cope with social anxiety and the fear of rejection. In his adult life, he continued to use sex to cope with problems and stress. Pornography became Larry's crutch and his shameful secret.

Larry's addiction continued after marriage. Many addicts hope marriage will be the solution to their problem because of the availability of sex. Sometimes this does help, and the addiction lays dormant for a while. But in other cases, the addict "brings the addiction" into the marriage and learns to hide it rather than confront the problem.

Larry was afraid of exposing his secret life. Fearing social criticism and judgment, he hid behind the anonymity of the computer. When he became bored with pornography, he found chatrooms. This was an exciting discovery. As he justified his actions, his addiction escalated. When Larry's wife caught him, the walls hiding his addiction came tumbling down. The secret was out of the bag. It was time to look into the mirror and face reality.

Larry's story is one of strength and courage as well as pain and failure. It takes courage to admit to a problem and face it directly. Larry was willing to share his story with others. He went to counseling, found a twelve step-recovery support group, and sought spiritual guidance from his pastor—all necessary steps for recovery to take place. The first step was admitting he had a problem. Taking this courageous first step led Larry on a journey of exploration and healing. His new motto is "No more secrets."

The Cycle of Sexual Addiction

In his 1983 book *Out of the Shadows,* Patrick Carnes advocated for the concept of sexual addiction as a recognizable and treatable problem.[1] He went on to write additional books that helped to explain the complexities of sexual addiction. Carnes believed that sex could become an addiction for some people, just as drugs and alcohol become an addiction for some people. Like other addictions, sexual addiction bears four hallmarks: It builds tolerance. It produces withdrawal. It follows obsessive-compulsive patterns. And it produces shame.

Moreover, Carnes determined six warning signs to determine whether sex has become an addiction: Addictive sex is done in isolation. Addictive sex is secretive. It is devoid of intimacy. It is devoid of relationship. It is victimizing. And it always ends in despair.

As Carnes studied sexual addiction, he noted that it progressed through four levels:

- Level 1: the addict uses fantasy, pornography, and masturbation to achieve a high (that is, sexual release).

- Level 2: the addict needs live pornography to provide release. He also may develop a fetish and seek sex outside of marriage to feed his high.

- Level 3: the addict's growing drive may lead to minor criminal offenses, prostitution, voyeurism, and/or exhibitionism. If he does not seek help at this point for his addiction, he will progress to level 4.

- Level 4: the addict is likely to face severe legal consequences for molestation, incest, and/or rape.

Carnes used these words to describe the cycle of sexual addiction: *obsession, the hunt, recruitment, gratification, return to normal, justification, blame, shame, despair,* and *promises.*

Support Groups for Sexual Addicts

The 1980s gave birth to the support group movement as a way of acknowledging and combating sexual addiction. Support groups use a twelve-step recovery model very similar to Alcoholics Anonymous (see sidebar on p. 226). Group members are referred to as "recovering addicts" and follow the twelve-step philosophy. They share stories of success and struggles and encourage others to share in an open, nonjudgmental environment. These groups are not run or

What Is Sexual Addiction?

Several conceptual models have been developed to understand sexual addiction. Mark Griffiths[2] identified six core components of addiction, including the following:

Salience. Internet sex becomes the most important activity in the person's life and dominates his or her thinking (preoccupations and cognitive distortions), feelings (cravings), and behavior (deterioration of socialized behavior). For instance, even when not actually engaged in Internet sex, the person will be thinking about the next time.

Mood modification refers to the subjective experience (an arousing "buzz" or "high" or paradoxically tranquilizing feeling of "escape" or "numbing") people report having as a consequence of engaging in Internet sex. It is often viewed as a coping strategy.

Tolerance is the process whereby increasing amounts of Internet sex are required to achieve the former mood modification effects. This means the person gradually builds up the amount of the time spent in front of the computer engaged in Internet sex.

Withdrawal symptoms are the unpleasant feeling states and/or physical effects that occur when Internet sex is discontinued or suddenly reduced; for example, the shakes, moodiness, or irritability.

Conflict refers to conflicts between Internet users and those around them (interpersonal conflict), conflicts with other activities (such as a job, social life, hobbies, or interests), or conflicts within themselves (intrapsychic conflict and/or subjective feelings of loss of control) concerned with spending too much time engaged in Internet sex.

Relapse is the tendency for repeated reversions to earlier patterns of Internet sex—even the most extreme patterns typical of the height of excessive Internet sex—after many years of abstinence or control.

managed by therapists or counselors; instead, group members are encouraged to take responsibility for their own addictive behavior and to recognize the value of relying on others and a "higher power" for fellowship and strength. Although the higher power is usually associated with some belief and perception of God, support groups are not affiliated with a specific denomination or faith community.

Sexaholics Anonymous (SA), Sexual Compulsive Anonymous (SCA), and Sex and Love Addicts Anonymous (SLAA) are popular recovery programs for sexual addiction.[3] Each has a website that identifies its philosophy of recovery and offers information on sexual addiction and contact numbers.

Celebrate Recovery

Pastor Rick Warren, author of *The Purpose Driven Life*, began a "Celebrate Recovery" ministry through his Saddleback Church in California.[4] The program can be used to help those who are addicted to sex. It identifies Jesus Christ as the specific and only Higher Power and outlines eight key recovery principles based on the Beatitudes. These principles include the following:

R = Realize I'm not God; I admit that I am powerless to control my tendency to do the wrong thing, and my life is unmanageable.

E = Earnestly believe that God exists, that I matter to him, and that he has the power to help me recover.

C = Consciously choose to commit all my life and will to Christ's care and control.

O = Openly examine and confess my faults to God, to myself, and to someone I trust.

V = Voluntarily submit to every change God wants to make in my life and humbly ask God to remove my character defects.

A Twelve-Step Model

The model used by Sexual Compulsive Anonymous identifies the following steps:

1. We admitted that we were powerless over the sexual compulsion, that our lives had become unmanageable.

2. Came to believe that a Power greater than ourselves could restore us to sanity.

3. Made a decision to turn our will and our lives over to the care of God as we understood God.

4. Made a searching and fearless moral inventory of ourselves.

5. Admitted to God, to ourselves, and to another human being the exact nature of our wrongs.

6. Were entirely ready to have God remove all these defects of character.

7. Humbly asked God to remove our shortcomings.

8. Made a list of all persons we had harmed, and became willing to make amends to them all.

9. Made a direct amends to such people wherever possible, except when to do so would injure them or others.

10. Continued to take personal inventory, and when we were wrong promptly admitted it.

11. Sought through prayer and meditation to improve our conscious contact with God as we understood God, praying only for knowledge of God's will for us and the power to carry that out.

12. Having had a spiritual awakening as the result of these steps, we tried to carry this message to sexually compulsive people and to practice these principles in all our affairs.

E = Evaluate all my relationships; offer forgiveness to those who have hurt me and make amends for harm I've done to others except when to do so would harm them or others.

R = Reserve a daily time for God; for self-examination, Bible readings, and prayer in order to know God and his will for my life, and to gain the power to follow his will.

Y = Yield myself to God to be used to bring the Good News to others, both by my example and by my words.

Scriptural Guidance for Recovery

In the beginning God created the heavens and the earth. Now the earth was formless and empty, darkness was over the surface of the deep, and the Spirit of God was hovering over the waters.

And God said, "Let there be light," and there was light. God saw that the light was good, and he separated the light from the darkness. God called the light "day," and the darkness he called "night." And there was evening, and there was morning—the first day.

And God said, "Let there be a vault between the waters to separate water from water." So God made the vault and separated the water under the vault from the water above it. And it was so. God called the vault "sky." And there was evening, and there was morning—the second day.

And God said, "Let the water under the sky be gathered to one place, and let dry ground appear." And it was so. God called the dry ground "land," and the gathered waters he called "seas." And God saw that it was good.

Then God said, "Let the land produce vegetation: seed-bearing plants and trees on the land that bear fruit with seed in it, according to their various kinds." And it was so. The land produced vegetation: plants bearing seed according to their kinds and trees bearing fruit with seed in it according to their kinds. And God saw that it was good. And there was evening, and there was morning—the third day.

And God said, "Let there be lights in the vault of the sky to separate the day from the night, and let them serve as signs to mark seasons and days and years, and let them be lights in the vault of the sky to give light on the earth." And it was so. God made two great lights—the greater light to govern the day and the lesser light to govern the night. He also made the stars. God set them in the vault of the sky to give light on the earth, to govern the day and the night, and to separate light from darkness. And God saw that it was good. And there was evening, and there was morning—the fourth day.

And God said, "Let the water teem with living creatures, and let birds fly above the earth across the vault of the sky." So God created the great creatures of the sea and every living and moving thing with which the water teems, according to their kinds, and every winged bird according to its kind. And God saw that it was good. God blessed them and said, "Be fruitful and increase in number and fill the water in the seas, and let the birds increase on the earth." And there was evening, and there was morning—the fifth day.

And God said, "Let the land produce living creatures according to their kinds: livestock, creatures that move along the ground, and wild animals, each according to its kind." And it was so. God made the wild animals according to their kinds, the livestock according to their kinds, and all the creatures that move along the ground according to their kinds. And God saw that it was good.

Then God said, "Let us make human beings in our image, in our likeness, so that they may rule over the fish in the sea and the birds in the sky, over the livestock and all the wild animals, and over all the creatures that move along the ground."

So God created human beings in his own image, in the image of God he created them; male and female he created them.

God blessed them and said to them, "Be fruitful and increase in number; fill the earth and subdue it. Rule over the fish in the sea and the birds in the sky and over every living creature that moves on the ground."

Then God said, "I give you every seed-bearing plant on the face of the whole earth and every tree that has fruit with seed in it. They will be yours for food. And to all the beasts of the earth and all the birds in the sky and all the creatures that move on the ground—everything that has the breath of life in it—I give every green plant for food." And it was so.

God saw all that he had made, and it was very good. And there was evening, and there was morning—the sixth day.

Thus the heavens and the earth were completed in all their vast array.

By the seventh day God had finished the work he had been doing; so on the seventh day he rested from all his work. Then God blessed the seventh day and made it holy, because on it he rested from all the work of creating that he had done.

—Genesis 1:1-2:3

In their book *Wrestling With Angels: What Genesis Teaches Us About Our Spiritual Identity, Sexuality, and Personal Relationships*, Naomi Rosenblatt and Joshua Horwitz write:

In this first creative burst, God displays all the loving concern of an ideal parent as He prepares the world for humanity's arrival. Establishing basic boundaries of order and predictability, He begins to build the safe and secure infrastructure that every infant must have to establish trust in her world. A child learns to trust through predictability and routine. As psychologist Erik Erikson pointed out, a newborn baby first learns trust through her own bodily systems. As she begins to breathe and sleep and digest her mother's milk, the predictable functioning of her body becomes an analogue of the rhythms of the outside world—the days, the seasons, the tides. Day by day the child grows to trust in these consistent patterns in her life. Over time she begins to smile in recognition of the benignly predictable world around her.

To fulfill our potential as human beings we all need a modicum of order in our physical environment. The first thing a social worker tries to create in a troubled child's home is order and routine. Without a few fixed points in his daily life—dinnertime, bedtime, a parent at the breakfast table or waiting when he comes home from school—a child can't trust and learn and grow. Neither can an adult.

In the first day of creation, God creates order out of chaos. He creates light to balance the darkness. And he creates time by establishing a predictable progression from darkness to light, from evening to morning. This simple fact of life on earth—that the planet rotates regularly on its axis, that after every midnight there will be a dawn—gives order and stability to both our physical and spiritual existence. Every child who is frightened of the dark clings to this predictable truth. A Hebrew morning prayer praises God as "the One who renews creation every day." Each day's dawn renews our connection to the Creator and offers us the promise of a new beginning.[5]

Cybersexual addiction leads to personal and family chaos. There are very real consequences for straying from God's plan and purpose. The entire spiritual life of a person who is addicted to sex spins out of control. But there is hope: God continues to create order out of chaos.

As you read through the text from Genesis 1 and 2, notice the pattern within the verses. Notice how the writer used repetition to emphasize and punctuate the beauty of the process of creation. Each day concludes with "And there was evening, and there was morning—the first day." And the second day. And the third and the fourth, fifth, and sixth days. Each stage of creating order out of chaos is proclaimed a day. And it was good. But notice the absence of such repetition for the seventh day.

Is it possible that the ancient writers were helping us understand that God continues to be involved in our world and in our lives?

The Genesis story of creation demonstrates how God created order out of chaos. And that creative, redemptive power is still available to those who believe in him. The God who created the heavens and the earth can help you create order out of your personal chaos.

Strategies for Recovery and Change

The first step in healing and recovery is admitting to the problem. This may also be the most difficult step to take. Shame and embarrassment, failure to understand the destructive nature of cybersexual behavior, and resistance to breaking the pattern of addiction keep many people from taking this important step toward change. Admitting a problem takes courage and builds character. It leads to taking responsibility for one's actions. People are more likely to change when they recognize the problem and are motivated to fix it—the stronger the motivation the better.

Changing habits or patterns that have developed over a long time is hard work. People may experience self-doubt, a tendency to give up, and a fear of failure. It can be easy to give up in the face of adversity. Because the craving to satisfy sexual desire is powerful and intoxicating, breaking habits is a daily battle, and often there are relapses. Fortunately, there is a way to attack this problem and win the battle. Larry's experience illustrates the keys to victory.

Developing a Game Plan

Prayer. Larry was encouraged to pray on a daily basis for healing and spiritual renewal—including praying every time he felt the desire to sexually act out. It was a comfort for him to know he had a powerful weapon at his disposal. As he experienced the power of prayer, he developed a routine of starting and ending each day with prayer and personal reflection. This helped him get the day off to a good start and relax before bedtime. It gave him confidence that he could face any temptation that came his way.

Spiritual guidance. Larry sought spiritual guidance from his pastor. He began reading daily devotions and other material designed to grow his spiritual life. Following his pastor's advice, he contacted a Christian counselor who was experienced in treating sexual addiction. Larry became more active in the church and joined a men's Bible study and prayer support group. He was supported and encouraged by a powerful team of believers.

Counseling. Going to see a counselor was a very big step for Larry. He had always believed he could solve his own problems, and he was used to keeping his innermost thoughts and feelings to himself. Although he was nervous at first, once he began to establish rapport and trust with his counselor, he began to relax. The counselor explained that the purpose of counseling was to talk about and understand as much as possible Larry's addiction to pornography. From there they would work to develop tools for controlling these desires.

Larry began to feel confident that he could change. Talking openly and honestly about personal issues was hard work and at times emotionally painful, but gradually Larry experienced the power of expressing himself. He admitted he was afraid of opening old emotional wounds from his past. He had been living with a great deal of hurt and pain, but over time he began to feel better.

Through counseling, Larry learned how his curiosity about pornography escalated over time into a habit and addiction. He then focused on identifying all the possible triggers in his life (personal and situational) that made him want to engage in cybersexual behavior. He discovered that stress was a major trigger, including financial and work pressures. He worried about whether he could adequately provide for his family, and whether or not he would still have the same job in the next few years. He learned more effective ways of recognizing and coping with his stress, such as talking about what bothered him instead of bottling up his feelings and lashing out in anger. Once he became more skilled at recognizing the early warning signs of mounting stress levels, he reacted more quickly to gain control of it. He learned new ways of coping instead of using cybersexual behavior as a crutch.

Ten Keys to Successful Counseling

1. Find a Christian counselor with expertise in the field of sexual addiction.

2. Trust the counselor for guidance and advice.

3. Have a positive attitude about getting help.

4. Be motivated to change, and sustain the motivation over time.

5. Tell the truth. If you are tempted to relapse or you have relapsed, tell the counselor.

6. Follow through on homework assignments. They are designed to facilitate change.

7. Use and apply insight and self-awareness on a daily basis. They can be invaluable tools.

8. Practice techniques and interventions suggested by the counselor.

9. Work to strengthen your marriage and family.

10. Work to strengthen your spiritual life.

Larry took a break from the computer. To remove the temptation, he stopped using the computer altogether for a while. For those who need the computer for work, this may be difficult to do. In that case, it is extremely important to work with an accountability partner and use computer software that will let your partner know if you have visited a pornography website. Another option is to install software that blocks pornographic images altogether.

Larry followed the motto of taking one day at a time. He counts every good day, every temptation that is resisted, as a victory. Although he knows there will be many temptations to relapse, there are also opportunities for change and success.

Every desire to turn on the computer and look at pornography that is thwarted is a win. And each win is a building block toward personal growth and maturity. Over time the desire to use pornography will decrease.

Larry also attended a support group designed to assist men and women who are in recovery from sexual issues. He found the group to be very helpful as he learned from others' experiences and realized that he was not alone in his suffering.

A Pastor's Perspective

Larry came to me a broken man. When he told me he had a problem with Internet pornography, we immediately prayed for forgiveness and healing. I referred Larry to a counselor I knew who dealt with this type of problem. The counselor confirmed that Larry had an addiction to pornography and began to develop a treatment plan for him. A group of men from our church and I became Larry's accountability and prayer partners. Together we helped Larry refocus his spirituality. This proved invaluable to Larry's recovery.

Questions for Reflection and Discussion

1. How can sex become addictive?

2. What role do masturbation and sexual fantasy play in developing a sexual addiction?

3. What light does the story of God's creation out of nothing shed on our ability to recover from sexual addiction?

4. Many people who struggle with a sexual addiction find support for recovery in twelve-step programs modeled after Alcoholics Anonymous. Perhaps your small group could explore whether such resources are available in your community and consider whether your church could sponsor such a program, if there is a need.

Notes

Chapter 1

1. Alexa Research (2001). "Alexa Research finds 'sex' popular on web." *Business Wire,* February 14, 2001.

2. Cooper, A., D. Delmonico, and R. Burg (2000). "Cybersex users, abusers, and compulsives: New findings and implications." In A. Cooper (Ed.), *Cybersex: The Dark Side of the Force* (pp. 5-29). Philadelphia: Brunner-Routledge.

3. Focus on the Family (2000). "Zogby survey reveals a growing percentage of those seeking sexual fulfillment on the Internet." Retrieved from the World Wide Web on March 1, 2003: www.pureintimacy.org/news/a0000031.html.

4. Schlosser, E. "The Business of Pornography." *U.S. News & World Report* (Feb. 10, 1997): 42.

5. Cited in "Archive of Statistics on Internet Dangers, Enough Is Enough." Retrieved from the World Wide Web on October 26, 2008: www.enough.org.

Chapter 2

1. MSNBC/Stanford/Duquesne Study, *Washington Times*, January 26, 2000.

2. Ibid.

3. Ropelato, Jerry (2007). "Internet Pornography Statistics. Internet Filter Review." Retrieved from the World Wide Web on October 26, 2008: http://internet-filter-review.toptenreviews. com/internetpornography-statistics.html

4. Cooper, A. (2000). "Cybersex users, abusers, and compulsives: New findings and implications." In A. Cooper (Ed.), *Cybersex: The Dark Side of the Force* (pp. 5-29). Philadelphia: Brunner-Routledge.

5. Grundner, Tom (2000). *The Skinner Box Effect*. Lincoln, Nebraska: Writers Club Press.

Chapter 3

1. Steketee, Gail, Teresa Pigott, and Todd Schemmel (2003). *Obsessive Compulsive Disorder: The Latest Assessment and Treatment Strategies*. Kansas City, Mo.: Compact Clinicals.

Chapter 4

1. Cooper, A. (2000). "Cybersex users, abusers, and compulsives: New findings and implications." In A. Cooper (Ed.), *Cybersex: The Dark Side of the Force* (pp. 5-29). Philadelphia: Brunner-Routledge.

2. Schneider, J. P. (2000). "Effects of cybersex addiction on the family: Results from a survey." In A. Cooper (Ed.), *Cybersex: The Dark Side of the Force* (pp. 31-58). Philadelphia: Brunner-Routledge.

3. Quittner, J. (April 14, 1997). "Divorce Internet style." *Time*, 72.

4. Smedes, Lewis (1984). *Forgive and Forget: Healing the Wounds We Don't Deserve*. San Francisco: Harper San Francisco.

5. Ibid.

6. Flanigan, Beverly (1992). *Forgiving the Unforgivable: Uncovering the Bitter Legacy of Intimate Wounds*. New York: Collier Books.

7. Adapted from Flanigan's model of reciprocal forgiveness and reconciliation.

8. National Institute of Mental Health (2007). "Depression." Retrieved from the World Wide Web on August 15, 2007: http://www.nimh.nih.gov/healthinformation/depressionmenu.cfm.

Chapter 5

1. Sharf, Richard S. (1996). *Theories of Psychotherapy and Counseling: Concepts and Cases*. Pacific Grove, Calif.: Brooks/Cole Publishing Company.

2. Cooper, A., D. Delmonico, and R. Burg (2000). "Cybersex users, abusers, and compulsives: New findings and implications." In A. Cooper (Ed.), *Cybersex: The Dark Side of the Force* (pp. 5-29). Philadelphia: Brunner-Routledge.

3. Schneider, J. P. (2000). Effects of cybersex addiction on the family: Results from a survey. In A. Cooper (Ed.), *Cybersex: The Dark Side of the Force* (pp. 31-58). Philadelphia: Brunner-Routledge.

4. Sharf, Richard S. (1996). *Theories of Psychotherapy and Counseling: Concepts and Cases*. Pacific Grove, Calif.: Brooks/Cole Publishing Company.

Chapter 7

1. Whealin, J. (n.d.). "Child Sexual Abuse." National Center for PTSD Fact Sheet. Retrieved from the World Wide Web on March 26, 2006. http.//www.ncptsd.va.gov/ncmain/ncdocs/fact_shts/fs_child_ sexual_abuse.html?opm=1&rr=rr1747&srt =d&echorr=true.

2. Kraizer, S. (1996). "Sexual Abuse." The Safe Child Program. Retrieved from the World Wide Web on March 21, 2006: http://safechild.org/childabuse1.htm#Indicators%20of%20 Sexually%20Abusive%20 Parent/Guardian.

3. Darkness to Light (2007) "Statistics Surrounding Child Sexual Abuse." Retrieved from the World Wide Web on August 27, 2007: www.darkness2light.org/KnowAbout.

Chapter 8

1. Frank Stanley can be contacted at: Frank Stanley, P.C., Attorney at Law, 200 North Division Avenue, Grand Rapids, Michigan 48503.

2. Operation Innocence Online (2006). Retrieved from the World Wide Web on June 26, 2006: http://innocenceonline. com/statistics-main.asp.

Chapter 9

1. Operation Innocence Online (2008). Retrieved from the World Wide Web on October 26, 2008: http://innocenceonline. com/statistics-main.asp.

Chapter 10

1. Carnes, P. (1983). *Out of the Shadows: Understanding Sexual Addiction.* Minneapolis: Compcare.

2. Griffiths, Mark (2000). "Does Internet and Computer 'Addiction' Exist? Some Case Study Evidence." *Cyberpsychology & Behavior*, 3(2): 211-218.

3. For more information about these recovery support groups, go to www.sa.org, www.sca-recovery.org, and www.slaafws.org.

4. For more information go to www.celebraterecovery.com.

5. Rosenblatt, Naomi and Joshua Horwitz. (1995). *Wrestling with Angels*. New York: Delacorte Press.